Akua Rugg

ATS

TS

ritique
e Film

RACE TODAY PUBLICATIONS

First Published 1984
by Race Today Publications
165 Railton Road, London SE24 0LU
Typeset and designed by RT Studios
Printed by Blackrose Press
©Race Today Collective
All rights reserved
Paperback ISBN 0 947716 00 9

For Darcus Howe

Acknowledgements: I would like to thank John La Rose who first suggested that I should present my work for publication; Farrukh Dhondy and Linton Kwesi Johnson who always made themselves available to discuss matters with me, and CLR James who not only gave me the run of his library but filled many gaps in my knowledge by answering my questions. Thanks also to members of the Race Today Collective who previewed my reviews.

CONTENTS

INTRODUCTION

I have been reviewing the arts for almost a decade now in the journal *Race Today*. Writing for *Race Today* is an extension of my long-standing interest in the arts.

As a child I read voraciously. My early childhood thrills were provided by the fairy tales of The Brothers Grimm, Hans Anderson and the myths of the Ancient Greeks and Romans rather than 'video nasties'. I read the classics: Beatrix Potter, Allison Uttley, Edward Lear, E. Nesbit, Francis Hodgson Burnett, Robert Louis Stephenson, Louisa M. Alcott, C. Day Lewis, Kenneth Grahame, H.G. Wells, J.M. Barrie, Christina Rossetti, George Macdonald, The Brontes, and Jane Austen. All these authors stimulated my imagination. I enjoyed contemporary authors like Noel Streatfield and the historical novels of Georgette Heyer. I was intrigued and baffled by Laurence Durrell's *The Alexandria Quartet*. For light relief I turned to comics — *Dandy, Beano, Schoolfriend* and the rather more staid publications like *The Children's Newspaper* and the glossy children's literary magazine *The Young Elizabethan*. I was amazed to discover, aged 11 that the authors of the musical *My Fair Lady* had pinched their storyline from Shaw's *Pygmalion*, for as children we were always taught that copying other people's work was a cardinal sin.

I attended 'Saturday Morning Pictures' religiously. I particularly liked 3D films and the give-away specs that went with them. My enjoyment of these sessions was somewhat marred by the Tarzan films and westerns which were staples of the programmes. I came from Africa and objected to the way the 'natives' were portrayed. Furthermore, I always wanted the Indians to kill the cowboys.

I enjoyed art classes at school, and found the art room a welcome refuge from the regular classrooms with the attendant horrors of algebra and the like. I spent happy

7

hours looking at reproductions of the classical painters: El Greco, Velazquez, Goya, Vermeer, Van Gogh, Gaugin, Matisse and Seurat. I used to pore over a column in an art periodical called 'Pictures in Disgrace'. It featured works by artists such as Manet whose pictures had apparently shocked the art establishment of the time, although the works seemed pretty conventional to me.

My favourite subject of all was drama. Through my drama classes I was exposed to a much wider range of literature than appeared on the school syllabus. I studied the work of the 'metaphysical' poets, the 'Restoration' playwrights as well as modern playwrights like Jean Anouilh. End of year school competitions when the various 'houses' fielded theatrical productions, gave the opportunity of directing as well as acting. My directorial debut, a stage adaptation of *Little Women*, was marked by controversy. Despite the fact that my actors were prompted in a loud voice (I was taking no chances) by me from the wings, and I made several unscheduled appearances on stage ferrying forgotten props to and fro, the production had the audience rolling in the aisles. It was awarded first prize. There were mutterings from my rivals about my playing to the gallery and lowering artistic standards. As far as I was concerned the critics could go hang, it was the audience's response I cared about. Because of the low timbre of my African voice I was usually cast in a male role — parts at the all girl school I attended being allocated on the basis of 'heavy' and 'light' voices. I trod the boards as Hamlet, Hercules and Pharoah, secretly fancying myself as Ophelia, Ondine and Cleopatra. I liked drama because it took literature beyond the academic confines of the printed word. My drama teacher was the legendary, Bristol-based elocutionist, Eileen Hartley-Hodder. I can remember the junior choral verse troupe, of which I was a member, bending with one knee to duck the collected works of some illustrious author. Miss Hodder had hurled the tome at us when, after weeks of rehearsal, a section, missing a cue, chimed in at the wrong moment during a stirring rendition of James Elroy Flecker's *The Golden Journey to Samarkand*. So if my judgements at times seem harsh, bear in mind that I was raised in a tough school of criticism.

I grew up in the 50s and all the art I had knowledge of was Eurocentric. I only came across work of artists on an

international scale after I left school. I was first introduced
to the work of black writers by Christopher Okigbo, the late
Nigerian poet. He gave me a batch of books which included,
in addition to works by Dorothy Richardson and Virginia
Woolf, a book of short stories by 'coloured' South African
author Richard Rive, James Baldwin's book of essays *The
Fire Next Time* and poems by Saint John Perse from Guade-
loupe. It wasn't only in literature that I made new discov-
eries. Never much interested in classical ballet, I was enthused
by the work of dance innovators like Martha Graham. I
attended dance classes given to amateurs by the London
School of Contemporary Dance. I met Christopher Bruce,
leading dancer and choreographer with the Ballet Rambert.
He told me it had been a toss up between his becoming a
ballet dancer or footballer. He invited me to watch rehearsals
of the company. When African American Alvin Ailey brought
his dance company to London, I was able to appreciate the
discipline and technique behind the seemingly effortless
grace and natural vigour of the dancers. In the visual arts I
was getting my eye in on modern painters like the 'pop'
artists; Richard Hamilton from Britain and Jasper Johns
from America. I saw avant garde theatrical productions,
among them Peter Brook's production of the play *Marat-
Sade* for the Royal Shakespeare Company. This was a play
within a play about the death of Marat enacted by the
inmates of a lunatic asylum. At the Roundhouse, London's
leading venue for 'alternative' theatre, I saw a production
by the French company, Le Grand Magic Circus. They
presented a Christmas pantomime quite unlike any other,
with a crucifixion taking place on stage! The films I saw
at this period bore little resemblance to those produced
by the Hollywood factory. There were films directed by
Godard from France, Pasolini from Italy and Bunel from
Spain. There were also 'political' films from South America -
Hour of the Furnaces a film about the anti-colonial struggles
of Argentinian workers by Fernando Solanas and the films
of Brazilian, Glauber Rocha, whose work examined the
possibility of an authentic cinema in third world countries.

My joining the Race Today Collective in 1974 and writing
for the journal brought me into contact with the work of
artists from Africa, Asia, the Caribbean and America and
opened another window for me on the world of art. I
brought to bear on what I now read, saw and heard critical

faculties that had been developed through my appreciation of Eurocentric art.

There was a striking difference between the art I'd previously interested myself in and the works I and others reviewed in the pages of *Race Today*. Art in Britain today seems to me to be fossilised in the state museums, art galleries, theatres and cinemas which are not supported by the mass of people. On the other hand 'the food for thought' provided by television, the commercial theatre and cinema and the popular press is a 'junk diet' of trivia which diverts rather than focuses people's attention on issues that are of vital concern to them. The arts we in *Race Today* concern ourselves with are characterised by vibrancy and vitality. They are the artistic and cultural expression of struggles being waged by peoples for liberation, whether from economic, political, racist or sexual oppression; of people demanding changes in the old social relationhsips and seeking ways to bring about change and progress. Let me give you an example. In *Race Today* we have reviewed the work of African-American writers Alice Walker, Toni Morrison, Ntozake Shange, Rosa Guy and that of the Jamaican theatre company, Sistren. The work of these artists gives a voice to women in the societies they come from. It reveals their struggles which have hitherto been hidden and projects images of women who see themselves not as passive victims unable to change the circumstances of their lives but as protagonists willing and able to determine their own destinies.

When I first joined *Race Today* work produced by radical and black artists was a mere trickle. There was the odd play presented at the Keskidee Centre, at that time the only permanent venue for black plays. A film by a black director might surface at long intervals at the London Film Festival, only to sink shortly afterwards, seemingly without trace. This trickle has now become a deluge. The Black Theatre Cooperative has been set up providing writers, directors, actors and technicians with a base for perfecting their craft. Whilst they do not have permanent premises as yet, they have established themselves with a television series ensuring them a large following should they mount a production on stage. Plays by black authors are shown regularly at the more established 'alternative' venues, and last year a West End theatre ran a three month season of

10

'Black' theatre. There have been two major film festivals of non-European film at which the work of black film directors working in Britain have been exhibited, alerting those interested that a body of films by black film makers exists. Last year, Creation for Liberation, a Brixton-based cultural organisation, sponsored the first ever open exhibition of work by black artists. They collaborated in this enterprise with groups such as the Pan Afrikan Connection, a group of young artists working in the midlands and individual artists from all over the country. Creation for Liberation also holds regular seminars on all aspects of the arts, giving artists an opportunity to present and discuss their work. There are a number of independent and radical black publishing houses, three of which, over the last three years, have fielded an international bookfair of radical black and third world books which brings artists to Britain from all over the world, and affords them the opportunity of promoting their work.

Art and culture represent a storehouse for sorting and ordering ideas. Some of the material housed there will undoubtedly be lumber which can only be cleared by a sensitive and informed critical response to the work produced by artists. Our artists need our brickbats as well as bouquets if their works are to hit the heights.

Untogether

Together Black Women
by Inez Smith Reid
Published by Third Press £3.50

The express purpose of the book, according to its author Inez Smith Reid, was to 'spark serious debate about the future and direction of black people', and 'also to afford a basis for that kind of black social activism which can have a lasting' and 'deep impact in terms of erasing the oppression which is too familiar to black people'.

Of the 12,000,000 women who make up the black female population of America, 202 were chosen to be the subjects of the book, which would serve as an index of the degree of militancy within the group.

Although the formal task of the study was identifying, describing and locating within the wider community the significance of the way these black women dealt with their particular oppression, much useful information has been withheld. This is allegedly to protect the participants from unwelcome official attention. However, the book while paying lip service to the idea of black women emerging as a new and powerful force in the current struggle being waged by the less powerful sections of society, interprets their actions in a manner that does nothing to further the development of their struggle.

Ms Smith has at her disposal her own formidable intellectual training, a battery of social science techniques, and the support, moral, and financial, of the Black Women's Community Development Foundation. How has she exploited these resources? Firstly there was the question of the selection of participants. It seems that a 'reputation in the community for militancy' was the main criterion they had to satisfy. Ms Smith then spent hours of scholarly research which led her to a radical shift in the whole perspective of the study. Scurrying off to define the term militant with particular reference to the black community, she lights upon the word 'together' in a dictionary of Afro-

American slang. It is almost a mystic experience for her, she drops her initial brief and comes up not with the militant (a white concept) but the 'together' black woman. This glibness of approach characterises the whole style of the book. Thus a whole chapter is devoted to recounting Ms Smith's level of black consciousness, being raised by the scepticism and mistrust levelled against her by the subjects of her study.

From the evidence of the main body of the work, a reputation for being militant within the community rests not only on black women's opposition to the women's liberation movement, gross disenchantment with the infrastructure of the USA, espousal of violence as the final solution and critical appraisal of both white and black modes of political organisation. The 'together' black woman also has a capacity to 'run her mouth' on the variety of subjects Ms Smith interprets as being meaningful for black people. We are therefore given page after page of the sisters 'rapping' on: the women's movement, population control, the third world, Marxism, the Civil Rights and Black Power Movements.

Instead of at this point filling us in with the sort of hard facts that would have made these interviews meaningful in terms of the interviewees' relative positions within the system, we are treated to such gems as — 'a beautician from the East', — from the Mid-West, a believer in astrology', — 'A Westerner with a Phd'. Presumably this format is meant to convey to us the vitality and vigour of the women concerned, but the spoken word inevitably loses from its wholesale transference to another medium. And any sense of gutsy immediacy is lost by having continually to consult the statistical tables at the beginning of the book for the women's religious and political affiliations, their ages, and employment.

Ms Smith claims as another unifying characteristic of her sample, their reluctance to 'accept totally the value structure of the white community' — this being the case how does she justify the inclusion of women who accepted notions like black capitalism, the pathological weaknesses of black men etc. The Southern origins of the majority of the women, and their socio/economic positions perhaps reveal more about Ms Smith Reid's relationship to that structure than to the black community as a whole.

In order to qualify as a participant in the project the

'together black woman had to have her mind free of con-
fusion, to be positive, function and emerge as a whole (person). It is doubtful whether by these criteria Ms Smith
Reid's study merits the description 'together'.

There is without doubt a serious lack of material about
the significance of black women's autonomous organisation
against their oppression. We must however begin to differ-
entiate between material that helps us to develop the next
stage of the black movement, and those works, which serve
merely as potboilers for those trying to capitalise on the
power that the varying sections of the community win
for themselves when they move in their own interests and
on their own behalf.

August 1975

Women Under Apartheid

For Their Triumphs and Their Tears
by Hilda Bernstein
Published by International Defence and Aid
£0.50

The declaration of an International Women's year indicates, in some form, an acceptance of the idea that women, the world over, share specific forms of oppression. That South Africa should provide the background for an exposition of this political fact of life is entirely appropriate. This is shown in the book *For Their Triumphs and Their Tears*, a detailed account of the lives of black South African women.

'Women in South Africa suffer first and foremost from the disability of apartheid.

'South African society is built in layers in which class and colour coincide. The position of South African women corresponds to their skin colour. The white man is at the very top, at the very bottom of the pile is the black woman.'

The rise of industry in South Africa has been characterised by the development of the primary industries such as mining. A constant supply of cheap ie black labour is therefore essential to the maintenance of the present system.

'Migrant labour from other countries releases local men to work on the farms, in the factory and as domestic servants'.

But whereas black men can, because of their position in the labour hierarchy, exact from the state the basic necessities of food and shelter, women lack even this material base from which to organise.

In the resettlement areas, life for women reveals the government's total abdication of any responsibility for the lives of black women. Deprived of the wage the urban areas offer, a few women can expect financial assistance from men in the towns, but the vast majority are dependent on the scarce resources from the particularly unproductive land in the 'resettlement areas'. Resources which moreover are unequally distributed.

'By law, allotments of land may be made to any married person. . . who is officially a citizen of the particular reserve or 'homeland'. A widow or unmarried woman with family obligations can be defined as a 'kraalhead' but the allocation of land is an administrative act that cannot be challenged in a court of law. Only a widow with children has any chance of being allocated land, and usually she will receive only half of the allocation made to a man. The lack of job opportunities in the reserves and extreme poverty leads inevitably to sickness and death, and the Government does not keep full mortality or morbidity statistics for Africans as it does for all other sections of the population. . .'
In one reserve alone 400 children died in three years.

The independent organisation of women is chronicled not only by the roll call, at the back of the book, of the names of women who marched, demonstrated, were arrested and tortured; but also in the descriptions of the day-by-day organising of bus boycotts, and pass burnings, not to mention the organisation needed to make arrangements for their dependents.

Hilda Bernstein's book is timely for many reasons. It contributes to the current debate concerning the tendency of oppressed groups to organise autonomously. It fills the need there is for low cost books which marshal a great deal of information compactly. Information moreover, which is presented without incomprehensible jargon but explains in easily understood terms, the complex political system that maintains apartheid in South Africa.

September 1975

16

Positive Images

Pressure: A Film Directed by Horace Ove

It is a notoriously difficult enterprise to deliver a film, sound in thought and action, from the initial gleam in the mind's eye of the film maker, to the end product, emerging from the darkness of the cinema auditorium. Nevertheless, the 1975 London Film Festival saw the premiere of the first full length feature film in Britain — inspired, scripted, directed and acted in the main by black people.

Pressure is the title of the film and pressure its theme. The film centers around the attempt of a British born West Indian teenager to secure a job commensurate with the 'O' level certificates he holds. His failure to do so allows director, Horace Ove, to show the reactions of family, friends and prospective employers to the youth's predicament.

He is an unemployed youth, but not of the unemployed youth. The camera follows him, as he makes his way to unite with that independent social grouping within the black community — the thousands of young wageless blacks in major cities — the urban guerillas. In seeking to identify that process, Ove gets lost in so much of the detail of other sections of the society. Though important in themselves, and as such subjects for separate films, they appear to intrude upon and distract from the particular experience the film sets out to evoke.

Ove is a pioneer, in that he is attempting, for the first time, to use the medium of film to reveal the inner soul of the black condition in Britain. He could not resist the temptation to propagandise against the white population's total lack of understanding of the black community.

In order to achieve this aim, Ove employs a technique that is neither the probing journalism of the documentary nor the sharp sting of the drama, with the result that the film is wedged between both. The characters suffer, because no-one is ever placed in a social and political context, nor is any single character sufficiently penetrated in depth. The camera flits from 'fish and chip man' Tony, with his Gary Glitter poster, to his older brother and would-be political mentor, eating avocado pears for breakfast, and favouring wall decorations which proclaim black rebellion.

The relationship between these two is never explored nor explained, merely identified. To complete the former needs a film in itself. Then, both these adaptations of black life in Britain are contrasted with the orderliness and discipline of hard working middle-aged parents — the early immigrants. Again this area lacked both penetration and documentation. A second film now presents itself. All these intense and moving experiences cloud the central dynamic of the movie — the meeting of two sections of the young black wageless, the 'O' leveller and the mass of sufferers.

Even with these shortcomings, the film quickens in pace and interest when it takes on intense dramatization, and we look into the lives of those black people who have totally rejected The British Way Of Life. By an imaginative, sensitive and evocative use of location, incident and selection of leading players, we are given a strong impression of the suspense, urgency, drama and humour that we traditionally expect from a feature film.

We follow the hero in his involuntary journey through political meetings in seedy youth clubs in an atmosphere of hip boy scoutery. We witness romantic encounters, and a zombie like passage through a holy roller church service. We are taken through the restrictive fog of British racism to a final confrontation with that constant factor of the black experience, the muggers in blue. No more Dixon of Dock Green.

Ove's choice of subject matter is not the soft option superficial assessment of the film might suggest. He has tried to integrate the minutiae of the documentary film with the larger ideas and events associated with a feature film. The film's major achievement is that such a coherent, intelligent and disciplined statement about the lives of blacks should have seen the light of the big screen, arguably the most important medium for mass culture in our times.

Subject as a director is to the restrictions of commercial

outlets, and pressure to conform to dominant cultural norms, Ove has had to work within certain limitations. Requiring, as film making does, vast resources of money, scarce technical skills and expensive hardware, without a grant of £15,000 from the British Film Institute, the free use of the expertise of white technicians, and the total commitment to the project of the actors, the film could not have been made.

Perhaps, the greatest pleasure of the film was being able to watch black actors allowed the freedom to interpret their roles with authenticity and accuracy. Remembered, particularly, are Oscar James with his air of cherubic menace, and the young hustlers who use the money they get from selling revolutionary papers for their own personal liberation movement. Dave Kinoshi in particular has great screen presence.

We get some of our experiences of the world from images around us. And if nothing else, Horace Ove's film provides us with these images, images we can ponder, accept or reject as being significant and relevant to our need to explain our existence.

December 1975

Conflicting Worlds

Sherry and Wine
by Jimi Rand, presented by the Temba Theatre Company
at The Theatre at New End, Hampstead

Just as dramatic art mirrors life, so black actors are finding,
in common with other black workers, that the most effective
way of realising their full potential at the present time, is
to organise independently of their white colleagues and
the existing theatre structure.

One group of black artists who have pursued this line of
action are the Temba Theatre Company. Formed in 1972,
under the artistic direction of Alton Kumalo, actor and
South African political exile, the company has established
a precedent of using professional actors and selecting plays
whose themes are of vital relevance to black people.

The company's latest production, a short two-act play
called *Sherry and Wine,* invites us to step inside the living
room of a West Indian family. The father is nostalgic for
the 'sweet life' back home, and his university educated
daughter has hopes of a brave new world in a multi-racial
Britain. The immigrant father and the British-born-and-bred
West Indian daughter have both to come to terms with living
in a Britain riddled with class and racial prejudice. Actor
and playwright Jimi Rand has attempted to deal with the
preoccupations of West Indians caught in this particular
situation.

The disciplined and controlled timing of actress Isabelle
Lucas as mother and Valerie Murray as her best friend,
enables the play to work at a level of sheer entertainment.
The pretensions of the former, and the scheming and meddling of the latter when the eldest daughter of the house
invites her boyfriend, a 'good catch', home for a family meal
provides a universally comic situation which the two women

20

make particularly Caribbean. This potential to create a truly Caribbean character is also evident in the author's conception and development of the character of Orlando, whose howls of disbelief and desperation when he is served ;English water soup' and 'bush' (salad), instead of his expected rice and peas, again depicts accurately a Caribbean type.

The Temba Theatre Company commands our attention and critical appraisal, for it is their avowed intention 'to give artistic expression to black culture.'

A precedent for the use of a traditionally western medium such as film, by non-western people to express their particular culture, has been set in present day Japan and India. It remains to be seen whether the Temba Theatre Company, and other groups like it, will be able to use the existing media available to artists and invest them with a black identity.

March 1976

Blacks in the Spotlight

The Fosters: London Weekend Television
Fridays at 7.30 pm
Bar Beach Prelude
by Bode Towande
Transistor Radio
by Ken Tsaro Wiva

For the first time in our presence here in Britain we blacks have been presented on television as having an independent social existence. Always, we come alive on television when whites hate us, love us or want to help us.

The first example of this new trend is *The Fosters*, an all black family-comedy series beamed out by a major TV network at peak viewing time. An all moving, walking, talking version of 'Happy Families'.

Mr and Mrs Foster, the immigrants, worry about their daughter's virtue, despair over their eldest son with his aspirations of becoming an artist, and encourage the younger one, a budding intellectual, to study his books.

The programme's producers' concession to the idea of blacks in Britain having a distinct and valuable social existence is merely a token. The programme lacks the courage of its producers' apparent convictions that Britain is a fully multi-racial, multi-cultural society. What we are presented with is a British adaptation of an American series about a black family.

The origins are particularly evident in the characterisation of the children who portray watered down versions of the cute, back-talking all American brat. The programme is saved from total disaster by the authority and authenticity the adult figures bring to their roles. This is due not only to their maturity as professional actors, but to the strength they are able to draw on of having had first hand experience of the Caribbean culture the series seeks to reflect. But however skilled an actor may be, he has a relatively passive role within a dramatic production and has to work within the limitations of the material available to him.

Why is it that the producers have chosen to adapt an American script to portray black family life when there are, in the black community here, such fine script writers?

There exists within the black community a powerful and creative cultural force, and a number of theatre groups have surfaced as part of this movement. A look at the work of one of these groups, The Black Theatre Workshop, reveals that it it not only as performers that blacks have a contribution to make.

The work of two Nigerian playwrights introduced the Black Theatre Workshop to London recently. *Bar Beach Prelude* by Bode Towande concerned the Nigerian authorities' inability to produce bread for its citizens and its capacity to deliver the circuses. The action revolves around the careers of three men who graduate from picking pockets to starring at 'the bar beach show', — Bar Beach being the location for the public executions staged by the military regime to maintain law 'n' order in the aftermath of the scramble for oil-rich 'Biafra'. The negotiations between the jailor and the prisoners (he for his dash [bribe], and they for a few last luxuries) underlined the play's theme that crime does not pay — if you get caught.

Transistor Radio by Ken Tsaro-Wiva explored the relationship between Basi and Alali. Possessing only secondary school certificates that can't be cashed for food or rent, we first meet them holed up, hiding out from the landlady on her end-of-the-month rampage, beer bottle in hand. When the rent collecting aid is inadvertently left behind, the couple are provided with a solution to their problems. 'Mr Heineken' cruises Lagos distributing transistor radios to the fortunate owners of 'empties', and the proceeds from the sale of the radio will keep them for months. Scheming and dreaming, they are rudely awakened by the arrival of a licensing officer. They must pay for a licence, or pay him off with a dash. Threatened with arrest for extortion, the officer makes off with the bribe, leaving behind a fake licence. Unable to play their radio, the couple listen to the voice of a hawker urging them to invest in

23

Niger-pool, the national lottery.

It would be simplistic to criticise *The Fosters* on the basis that white cultural forms do not and cannot explore and celebrate the black experience. The writers working with The Black Theatre Workshop are equally influenced by North American popular entertainment forms, but their work has a strength *The Fosters* does not, because they fully exploit the formula they are working from. What distinguishes the best situation comedy is the encapsulation of a whole world in the particularities of language and gesture. This Tsaro-Wiva achieves in *Transistor Radio*, in contrast to the parody of the black British social existence the episodes of *The Fosters* have so far shown.

May 1976

A Negative View

The Black House: an exhibition of photographs
by Colin Jones

In June, a leading art gallery in central London, The Photographers' Gallery, showed an exhibition of photographs
which is to go on tour nationally, about Harambee or the
Black House as it is known to its residents.

Life at this government funded youth project was recorded by a *Sunday Times* photographer, and some 66 of
the resulting photographs have been chosen to represent
the experience of the young men and women who hang
out at this 'refuge' for homeless and rootless young blacks.

Initially, the photographs make a tremendous impact.
There is the novelty of seeing images of blacks in such
concentration; images, moreover, that are presented so
seductively. The hugely blown up, impeccably mounted
photographs, almost tempt one into believing the show's
own publicity that it is remarkable. Remarkable for what
and to whom?

The youths are lined up, posing in their stylish clothes,
lying in bed, sitting around smoking, playing cards and
sunning themselves back-a-yard. Occasionally they are
seen patching up the crumbling premises they have inheri-
ted.

Only two photographs suggest that the youth are more
than just the raw material for a photographic essay on a
rare and exotic phenomenon. In one of these photographs
we see prison letters sent by youths to Brother Herman,
founding father of the project. The second photograph shows
a room wrecked in 'an orgy of destruction'.

Are we seriously being asked to consider that black youth
have nothing more substantial to wrestle with than inanimate
bits and pieces of furniture?

The written texts, hanging alongside the photographs, express the youths' resistance and rebellion to the pressures they have to deal with. Why is this spirit not captured in the images presented in the exhibition? Hundreds of photographs must have been taken over the three years. What informed the process of selection that must have taken place for an exhibition of this stature?

The exhibition does not reveal the spirit and mood of a particular section of the black community at this point in their history. Rather, it reflects the colonial mentality of the establishment towards blacks in this country. The latter day explorer now ventures into darkest immigrant land armed with a camera. His penetration into this new territory is assisted by urban aid intermediaries.

The youths, captured on film, are mounted like so many trophies: spoils, which the race relations industrialists, project hatchers, not to mention idea-hungry editors of colour supplements can profit from.

Had the experience of the Black House been documented by those with an authentic interest in advancing the cause of the youth, it is unlikely that the overwhelming impression given by the exhibition would be that our youth are winsome, passive victims of circumstance, whose salvation lies in liberal well wishers propagandising on their behalf.

Those who check out the exhibition should bear in mind that there is more to a photographic image than meets the eye.

June/July 1977

Blacksploitation

A Review of Black Joy
Distributed by Hemdale International Films

Black Joy, a film about life in Brixton, London's black ghetto, is currently featured in a series of full-page advertisements publicising the Cinema International Corporation's latest offerings.

Norman Beaton, Guyanese star of the film, is shown twinkling alongside Paul Newman, Barbara Streisand, Michael Caine et al.

Plaza 2, the cinema housing the film, is no down-town flea pit or inaccessible art film theatre. Situated just off Piccadilly, it is ideally placed to catch the tourist trade or the native out for a night on the town. The black presence in Britain, it seems, is suitable material for 'packing 'em in' at the centre of the nation's cinema land.

In common with many who will see the film, its hero, Benjamin Ignatius Samuel Jones, is ignorant of Brixton's ways and manners. Flat of foot, pretty of face and slow on the uptake, he is summarily relieved of his innocence, wallet and virginity by a succession of stock characters: city slickers, seductive venal women, unsympathetic bureaucrats.

Much has been made of the fact that the film is not political, and merely provides an hour of good, dirty fun. The residents of Brixton are shown cussing, fighting, bedding down and messing each other over with monotonous regularity. Reggae and soul music provide a contrast to the drab physical environment of a decaying inner city area.

The documentary style used in the direction of the film, and the attention to detail, evident in the scenes shot on location, suggest that those responsible for the original concept of the film had set their sights on something more than sheer entertainment. Some passages in the film pay homage to certain aspects of Caribbean culture — its patois, ways of dressing moving and being. This aspect of the film is particularly strong in the scenes dealing with the reception of immigrants at their point of arrival, conditions in a church doss house and the hassle of collecting welfare money.

A film which, in the main, depicts blacks as making the best of a bad job, rather than seeking alternatives, is a political statement in itself. *Black Joy,* which is finally a product of white society, fully bears out that society's assumptions that blacks are at the bottom of the heap and likely to remain there. What else is there to infer from the lives of people who, from the evidence of the film use their energies for nothing more than acquiring casual sex, dope and flash cars.

Black Joy will no doubt delight those for whom it was made — white film audiences - for it cannot possibly have been made for black audiences. Blacks do not avoid films with exclusively white themes. Furthermore, the publicity campaign mounted to market the film, invites people in the form of a strip cartoon, 'to spend a night out in Brixton'. Who needs a written invitation to their own home?

The movie moguls have taken a liberty commandeering the word black for the title of their film. One only has to consider the transformation of the name Emmanuel into an international symbol describing a soft pornographic film to appreciate how other words could be similarly debased. 'Black' films have come to be associated in the minds of film goers with plots that have a strong element of sex, drugs and violence. *Black Joy* contains all these ingredients. It panders to white society's prurient interest in certain aspects of black social life. It provides light entertainment for whites, who after all have their own culture for serious consideration.

The film doesn't have much to offer the actors either. Their performances are stereotyped. The men rant and rave and the women simper. All, in true film tradition, are acted off the screen by child star, Paul Medford. His rendition of Shirley Temple is no mean feat given that he is male, black, and the script writers have provided him with dialogue that's as risque as any in the film.

January 1978

A Play

A Play by Robert Serumaga

The Keskidee Arts Centre in North London has consistently encouraged and supported little-known black writers. Its theatre-in-the-round provides a venue for the staging of their work, and is particularly suited to the presentation of drama that is not set in a traditional mould.

I found the latest play at the Keskidee difficult to view favourably. The playwright has indulged his own artistic whims instead of disciplining himself to present his analysis of the lives of a certain group of blacks in an easily comprehensible and attractive form.

The stage of Keskidee's theatre, which has no proscenium arch, is entirely appropriate for this play; the auditorium serving as the four walls of the room in which the action of the play takes place. As the play opens, we find Mutimukulu, a westernised African chief, sitting in the room on the anniversary of his wife's murder. Serumaga uses this circumstance to explore Mutimukulu's preoccupations. A phantasmagoria passes before us, revealing an Africa in transition. Traditional Africa is symbolised by two characters played by Imruh Caesar and Gordon Tialobi. Dressed in African robes they chant, drum, play a traditional African board game, and tell endless riddles. Modern Africa is represented by Witty Forde and David Haynes dresssd in western styled suits cut from African cloth. Unlike their traditional brothers they cannot while away their time, harassed as they are by the complexities of modern urban life. Neither of these worlds offer Mutimukulu refuge from his difficulties.

Serumaga, because he is dealing with topical themes, appears to associate modern forms of drama with a lack of coherence in the structuring of plays. Characters are given repetitive dialogue and perform actions which do little to develop the themes within the play. This dramatic tedium finally resulted in what one might charitably label participation drama. When Caesar and Tialobi on several occasions retire from the centre of action, and fall asleep on stage, some members of the audience might have interpreted this as symbolic of the fading away of old Africa. Others, appearing to take their cue from the actors, could be observed in attitudes which suggested that they were not as alert to what was going on around them as one might have expected in a place of public entertainment.

Rufus Collins, the director works as best he can with his material. Off-stage sound is used to great effect to suggest Mutimukulu is haunted not only by his wife, but also by a menacing world beyond the confines of his room. He has to render Serumaga's shifting scene of real and imagined characters so that the political and social issues the play touches on are not completely obscured. The uncertainties and terrors that have seized the mind of Mutimukulu have to be realised in dramatic form.

Support for the performing arts (with the exception of music) within the black community is fragile. Black artists run the risk of crushing it if they do not discipline themselves into presenting work, topical thought it might be, in a popular form. It is one thing for an audience to stretch its mind, it is quite another for it to stretch its collective mouth in the gaping yawns that seemed to be on the order of the day, the night I went to see A Play.

January 1978

Camerawork Reviewed

A review of Camerawork, published by Camerawork Publishing Collective. Price 40p.

'What are you taking pictures for?' This question was flung at a photographer, recording the violence that flared in Lewisham High Street, on August 13, 1977.

That day, the police, with considerable force and brutality, prevented members of an anti-racist campaign from blocking the route of the National Front — a British fascist organisation — in their attempt at a public show of strength through the streets of a depressed, working class area, in south London, where large numbers of blacks live. An area, moreover, in which the anti-racist campaign had been refused permission to stage a counter-demonstration.

Camerawork, a publication which provides a forum for photography and other forms of communication, was prompted by the demonstrator's question to devote its entire November 1977 issue to 'Lewisham'. This particular issue aims at a practical exploration of 'the application, scope and content of photography', using the events that occurred in Lewisham as its point of reference. It contains articles detailing the background to, and aftermath of the confrontation, including the full text of the speech made by the National Front's chairman in Lewisham, which was not reported in the national press. Also published are photographs of the battles in the High Street, the like of which, did not appear in the press. Finally, it contains in-depth interviews with six of the freelance photographers whose work appears in the issue.

The articles in *Camerawork* describe how the establishment media decried the attempt of the anti-racist campaign to melt the tip of the iceberg of British racism, and how photographs were used, extensively, to substantiate this editorial political position — a position that interpreted the events at Lewisham in such a way as to infer that the political importance of the occasion derived from the fact that the law and order of the land was threatened, not by those who sought to stir up racialism in this country, but, on the contrary, by those who sought to oppose this. The pictures in *Camerawork* unlike those of the national press, show the custodians of 'peace in our time', laying into the anti-racist demonstrators with relish, police horses, and strong arm tactics. They show that the composition of the demonstration, again unlike the impression given by the national press, was an amalgam of black and white young and old, male and female members of the community.

In its documentation of how the establishment media used photography to substantiate its own particular editorial line, Camerawork is systematic, comprehensive and lucid. When it moves towards speculating on the ways this tendency might be combatted and the strength of this opposition, it is on less firm ground. *Camerawork* appears to believe that there exists an embryonic group of 'politicised' photographers, whose sympathies lie with progressive political development. It finds, in the interviews conducted with the freelance photographers, answers of 'unexpected political toughness'. However, a close study of the interviews reveal that this political toughness is not seen to extend to the photographers' fundamental task of getting their work before the public eye. The photographers appear not to have cared what use was made of their photographs, and although some photographs were used by public bodies such as the Open University, and the Borough of Lewisham, they were also used by the establishment press, here and abroad for its own purposes. Indeed one photographer states that the National Front would probably be quite pleased with the photographs of themselves that appeared in the *Daily Telegraph*.

The interviews with the photographers merely promote their individual careers and show us, once again, how easy it is for professionals to dip a liberal toe into the swirling waters of radical political activity and fool themselves, and us, into believing they have taken a plunge.

February 1978

Tourist Trap

A film directed by Trevor D Rhone, Produced by Knuts Productions, Jamaica.

Every year Jamaica is visited by a plague of tourists. Dropping from the sky, they swarm onto the island's tourist belt hungry for sun, fun and sin. The film, *Smile Orange,* tells of the triumphs and tribulations of a certain section of the Jamaican population as it resists the seasonal onslaught.

At the Montego Bay hotel, where the film's action takes place, chaos reigns. The assistant manager, a brown skinned guy considered by his staff as 'a black jackass looking over a white-washed fence', finds himself under seige. He has to pacify the white guests and rally together the black staff who, instead of attending to their duties, use the hotel's facilities for their own purposes.

Miss 'B', a swanky switchboard operator, uses her position to inform the staff of management's every move. Joe, the cook, responsible family man and solid as a tank, cools out the situation when things get hot. Cyril, ex cane-cutter turned bus-boy, is expertly drilled in his official duties in the dining hall, and his unofficial duties as gigolo. They are all welded together as a force against the hotel's management, which wants to protect its power, and the tourists who want to protect their privileges. This force is led by Ringo Smith, head waiter and con-man extraordinary.

As the film progresses, Ringo emerges as hero of the film and organisational genius, mobilising the black staff and manipulating management and guests. By the end of the film, he has charmed and conned everyone into aiding and abetting his every manouevre to make a quick killing. He seduces the assistant manager's blonde bombshell of a wife. He sabotages the attempts of the jumped-up black lady social director, who tries to dragoon everyone into

33

having a good time. In a sequence of inspired high comedy, he even manages to get a formidable middle-aged white American matron to save his reputation, livelihood and life. This occurs when he is compelled to fill a breach of his own making, when the two non-swimming life-guards he has foisted on the hotel split at a crucial moment.

The distinguishing mark of this film is that it never insults our intelligence, only the pretensions of the characters it depicts. Although a rip-roaring comedy, it doesn't earn the laughs it gets cheaply. Whites may be the butt of many jokes, but exploitation and oppression are not seen as being the perogative of whites. Blacks who aspire to being a part of an exploitative and oppressive system are exposed for what they are.

This is a gem of a 'black' film. Rare for the mastery those responsible for the production have over their chosen medium, valuable for the insights it gives us about the situation it describes. *Smile Orange* identifies and observes a particular place and the way of life peculiar to its inhabitants. Nevertheless, this multi-faceted, cool, sharp and sparkling film will prove irresistible to anyone with heart, soul, guts, funnybone and last, but not least, mind in full working order.

March 1978

Reggae

A film directed by Horace Ove
Presented by Bamboo Records

Horace Ove's *Reggae,* which shares a double billing with *Smile Orange,* also focuses on a single aspect of Jamaican culture, reggae, the popular music of the island's urban masses.

Made seven years ago, the film centres on a Reggae Festival held at the Empire Pool, Wembley. Ove uses this event as a point of departure for a cinematic journey to find the roots of a music transplanted to the foreign cultural climate of Britain.

The film revives such golden oldies as Desmond Dekker, Millie (My-Boy-Lollipop) Small, Toots and the Maytalls, Bob and Marcia, John Holt et al. Ove, however, does not appear to believe that the music can be left to speak for itself. The artists' performances are therefore padded out with a series of interviews with disc jockeys, record company bosses and black activists. Some of these interviews, given the meteoric rise in stock of reggae on the international music market, are of historical significance. Again and again, the view is expressed that there was almost a cultural conspiracy on the part of those who control the media to keep reggae out of the mainstream, so that those wishing to listen to it had to struggle to do so. Other interviews, however, brought the film to a standstill, with, for example, an English disc jockey holding forth solemnly on the Yoruba and Ibo roots of reggae.

The sequences, which cut back to Jamaica, and show the economic and social conditions out of which reggae emerged, provide the most powerful and imaginative images within the film. Shots of working class Jamaicans, on the streets

35

and in the markets, are contrasted with those of white tourists at their leisure. One particularly stunning image occurs when Ove shows us a luxury hotel. Suddenly, the ornately wrought balconies, adorning the hotel's spanking white facade, multiply rapidly all across the screen, whilst a voice-over intones, 'Jamaicans love to serve, serve, serve'.

The direction of the sequences of the performers at work are straightforward documentary reportage, which allows one to concentrate on the individual artist. One is struck, immediately, by their physical appearance. We have Millie in a long brown wig and satin mini-dress singing about Enoch Powell. Bob and Marcia, neatly trimmed afros atop dashikis with creases all in the right places, have news for us, that: 'to be young, gifted and black is where it's at'. Desmond Dekker, spruce in gypsy neck-kerchief, high waisted pants and white lace blouse, sings of the plight of the Israelites, but not yet of the liberation of an exodus. They seem light years away musically, socially and culturally from the reggae stars of later years for whom they paved a way. No dreadlocks, no red, green and gold vestments are to be seen.

Seven years ago, from the evidence on film, reggae does not appear to have drawn its followers exclusively from the ranks of the young and the black. We see suited men, shielded against a hostile British climate by umbrellas, not wooly tams. Inside the hall, white, mini-skirted teeny boppers and their skin-head partners gyrate, all knock knees and furious shakings of hair. The film thus shows us how, at a certain stage in its development in England, white youths could relate to the music and its practitioners on a superficial level, without seeking, or needing to identify with it and them culturally, spiritually and socially, as do the black youth today who follow sound systems.

In his insertion of sequences from the original King Kong film, Ove shows an ironic and prophetic wit. Reggae has now broken out of the bounds set for it by the dominant culture in this country to assert its own power and creativity. By seeking with the film to both educate and entertain, Ove concentrates on education at the expense of entertainment. By doing so, he blunts the impact of a medium which is heavily dependent on action and vivid, visual imagery, rather than on static delivery of speech, which too much of the film contains.

However, this film, with its strengths and weaknesses, is extremely important. By informing us, as it does, of where we are coming from, it lends power to the increasingly dynamic, cultural movement that exists within the black community in this country.

March 1978

Mau Mau

Presented by the Sussex African Students   Association

The Trial of Dedan Kimathi is a play written by Kenyan writers Ngugi wa Thiong'o and Micere Githae Mugo. It deals with the capture, imprisonment and execution of a hero of the Kenyan war of liberation from British colonial rule. Since December 1977, Ngugi has been imprisoned by the Kenyan government, and as part of an international campaign for his release, the Sussex African Students' Association Drama Group mounted a production of the play.

In keeping with Ngugi's belief that literary work should speak to and for the mass of the people, the play has been modified by the students so that the revolutionary ideas of Kimathi, rather than the personal exploits of the man himself, dominate the play. The character of Kimathi appears only in the dock at his trial, and in the torture chamber. Characters, such as peasants, and urban dwellers, demonstrate the effect Kimathi's 'enormous organising capacities' had on their lives, enabling them to achieve their own liberation. Other characters such as white and black soldiers, black churchmen, businessmen, civil servants and politicians show how Kimathi's tactics disrupted the smooth transition of power from white imperialists to the equally oppressive and exploitative rule of black capitalists.

In attempting to hammer home the political message that it is the mass of people, rather than heroes, which ultimately revolutionises a society, the play tends to sacrifice art to politics. The characters in the play come over as mouthpieces for political slogans and rhetoric. There is no depth to the characterisation of the individuals who appear before us.

Although this weakens the dramatic power of the play, by reducing characters to archetypes, the play shows us

38

how the problems encountered by Kenyans at this point in their history are the same problems shared by all oppressed people struggling for power over their own lives. Thus we have the strong peasant woman raising the consciousness of a decadent town dweller who expends his energy beating his female relatives in the struggle for everyday survival, rather than fighting the common enemy that has created the dire conditions of their lives. We see Kimathi resisting the attempts of a slick black businessman to co-opt his revolutionary energy by pointing out to him that other black leaders have achieved their positions of authority by working within the system. Kimathi's dialogue with a black nun exposes the church's role as an agency of control and domination within the capitalist scheme of things. By reducing the characters to symbols and representatives of the various strata of Kenyan society, the director is able to take the artistic licence of having women play men's roles. Indeed the male character of Kimathi who is confined to the courtroom scenes is provided with a female alter ego who interacts with the other characters in the play mobilising and politicising them. Through her and other female characters, the revolutionary potential of women in changing society is demonstrated.

The students were denied the use of Sussex University's major cultural venue, the Garden Centre and had to make do with a church hall on the campus. The director makes good use of this limitation by turning the congregation/audience into the public gallery of the courthouse. This intensified the feeling that both audience and cast are participating in something more than an artistic event and are celebrating together the victory of the Kenyan masses.

The play itself does not achieve a complete fusion of art with politics, at least not for black audiences in Britain who may be unfamiliar with the Mau Mau era and the exploits of its heroes and heroines. However, the circumstances surrounding the staging of the play at this time remind us that art is as powerful a weapon as any in the struggle against oppression and exploitation, and that artists of the people such as Ngugi are as much a threat to repressive regimes, as are political leaders such as Dedan Kimathi.

A fear of the revolutionary potential of artistic expression on the part of the powers that be, does not appear to be a phenomenon peculiar to Kenya, as those responsible for the staging of the play discovered when the Sussex police attended the production. Someone had tipped them off that blacks had been seen with guns on the campus. It seems the idea of blacks in possession of mere symbols of power is enough to set in motion this society's forces of coercion against them.

May/June 1978

Launching Carnival '78

On Saturday, 1 July 1,500 people came to the Commonwealth Institute in uptown Kensington, to celebrate the official launching of Carnival '78 which will be held downtown in Notting Hill on August 27 and 28.

The Institute's building, prestigious showcase of Britain's links with her former colonial territories was transformed for the evening into a hothouse of music, song, dance, good food and flowing drink to facilitate the annual blossoming of the cultural and social power of West Indians, which comes to full flower on the streets of Ladbroke Grove, where the costume bands appear in all their glory.

As befits the largest cultural festival in Britain (an estimated quarter of a million people attended last year's Carnival), the evening was organised in a highly disciplined and efficient manner. After the payment of an entrance fee, which will go towards funds for the Carnival, Carnival enthusiasts were free to wander the spacious halls and tiered galleries of the institute. The first of many things to please the eye and gladden the heart, as one entered the central hall, was an exhibition of the costumes that are going to be worn by the bands taking part in this year's Carnival. The band Sukuya is working around a Zulu theme, Metronomes are disguising themselves as 'Visitors from Outer Space', 'Ebony are presenting an 'Oriental Fantasy'; Lion Youth are depicting the conditions faced by black youth in this society with their theme of 'Youth War'; and last, but not least, Race Today Renegades are forwarding 'Forces of Victory', an army decked out in all the colours of the rainbow.

The evening opened with Selwyn Baptiste, director of the Carnival Development Committee (CDC), welcoming the Carnival enthusiasts and expressing the wish that this year's Carnival should be the 'biggest and best ever' and, from the events which followed, this seems very likely.

Entire families, ranging from toddlers born in this country,

41

had come to be initiated by their Caribbean born parents into the cultural rites of their homeland. Everyone, old and young, 'jumped up' to music provided by the steelband, Metronomes. As the evening progressed, spectators were able to look down from surrounding galleries onto a central stage where Carnival artists displayed their various skills. The Trinidad and Tobago Dancers and Singers, in their dance dramas, mixed modern ballet techniques with the more traditional elements, Caribbean folk songs, and stick fighting. The Paddington Youth Steelband took the stage next. These youngsters, in their early teens, showed none of the alienation and separation from Caribbean cultural traditions, which is made so much of, as they 'beat pan' and 'jumped up' with confidence, skill and controlled energy.

Carnival is not an event which is sharply divided into actors and spectators, and this spirit was much in evidence as the guests at the launching, after watching the acts on stage, availed themselves of the facilities provided by the bars set up for food and drink. They jumped up non-stop, hands held high above heads, their enthusiasm urging on the steelbandsmen to even greater heights. When energy for dancing flagged, people turned to promenading along the galleries, talking and socialising, renewing friendships with West Indians from abroad passing through London. The evening ended with Carnival artists and enthusiasts flowing down from all corners of the hall onto the central stage to dance until the organiser, reluctantly, had to call a halt.

The evening proved that Carnival is not merely a two day spectacle that appears on the street by magic. Funds have to be raised, costumes and instruments designed and prepared, artists need to practise and rehearse, and Carnival enthusiasts informed of what is going on. All these needs for the development and promotion of the carnival movement were amply met on this occasion of the official launching of Carnival.

July 1978

Blazing a Trail

Empire Road, BBC2 television series, screened from October 31 to November 28. Produced by Peter Ansorge and directed by Alex Marshall.

Empire Road, the new weekly black TV serial launched by BBC2 amidst a flood of publicity, concerns the daily lives of West Indians and Asians who live in the same neighbourhood in Handsworth, Birmingham. It is scripted but not directed by a black person, and nearly all the characters are black.

Michael Abbensetts, Guyanese scriptwriter for the series, obviously believes that people rather than politics make the world go round and the ratings go up. *Empire Road* therefore concentrates on how the West Indians and Asians in the street relate to each other. Their relationship to white society does not come in for detailed examination.

The chief character in the series is Everton Bennett, a Guyanese immigrant, who, during the 20 years he has been living in Britain, has acquired a supermarket and four houses which he lets. His ambitions and frustrations provide the dynamic for the whole series. Thrifty, industrious and intolerant of life styles that differ from his own, Bennett finds that the life he has so carefully constructed for himself crumbles at the edges where it comes into contact with other members of his community.

For a start, there is his own family continually stabbing him in the back. Walter, his live-in brother-in-law, is responsible for letting his houses to undesirable tenants. In one house Asians have turned the front room into a mosque. In yet another, Bennett is choked both by the ganja fumes and by the fact that the tenants in this particular house are unemployed 'Rastas'. His teenage son Marcus has fallen for a pretty Asian neighbour much to the disgust of her father, and his wife's mother is planning to fly from Guyana to share his home for an indefinite length of time.

These subjects — the pursuit of money and sex, escapes from mothers-in-law and other natural disasters of life — are the stuff that any popular weekly TV serial is made of. However, the distinguishing characteristic of a serial such as *Empire Road* is its power to compel an audience to watch it, episode after episode. The audience is usually held captive because it identifies with the lives of the characters who people the series. This process of identification can only take place if both director and scriptwriter pay scrupulous attention to detail of speech, mannerism, dress and decor. This vital ingredient seems to me to be missing from *Empire Road*.

Certainly, West Indian and English viewers will find themselves in accord with Bennett's disparaging remarks about the Asian community. Bennett considers them ignorant heathens who do not realise a front room is a shrine in which TV rather than God is worshipped, Asian and English viewers will no doubt warm to Bennett's contempt for the situation of West Indian youth, their attitudes to work and peculiar way of dress.

Norman Beaton, the actor who plays Bennett, is a joy to watch, but *Empire Road* is not a one man show. In relation to him the other characters seem to be underdeveloped or marginal to the progression of plot in the series. Bennett's wife Hortense, appears to have no other function than to prove that the nuclear family is alive and well within the West Indian community and to provide Bennett with a mother-in-law. This character, when she arrives fresh from Guyana, does not appear to have a Guyanese accent, nor does she use Guyanese idioms. The young Rastas, an important section of the West Indian community, are made to seem ridiculous rather than rebellious, with one of them sporting a Little Richard wig. More seriously, the relationship between the West Indian and Asian community is focused through the romance between sharp talking 'sweet boy' Marcus and obedient and strictly brought up Ranjaana. This is surely an unlikely turn of events given the social patterns of West Indian youth and the cultural norms of Asian society. The success of a serial like *Empire Road* depends largely on its capacity to persuade an audience to suspend disbelief, not on its ability to strain the audience's credulity.

44

On the credit side. Abbensetts has broken with the tradition that blacks must be presented on TV as either mentally deficient or socially delinquent. There is evidence that characters such as the stuttering and seemingly ineffectual Walter, and the 'workshy' youth will, in succeeding episodes, challenge the supremacy of Bennett's ideas.

On the debit side, Abbensetts has not made the fullest use of the distinctive characteristics of the black community. Where are the verbal fireworks that fill the air whenever West Indians are gathered together? A few anti-Asian 'curry' jokes are no substitute for the creative and vivid use of language that West Indians are famous for. The overall impression given by *Empire Road* is that blacks are boring, conformist and complacent. Surely these are not the characteristics that distinguish the black community from any other section of British society today.

Empire Road is a trailblazer, in that it is a TV production that presents blacks as protagonists rather than mere foils for white characters. It is one, however, that on the evidence of the few episodes so far screened splutters rather than bursts with life. It is unfortunate also, that such a radical departure from the norms of British television broadcasting should have been made on BBC2, the TV channel popularly regarded as the one nobody watches.

January 1979

Lacking Flair

Masada, written by Edgar White, directed by Rufus Collins. Performed at Keskidee from October 26 to Novmber 12.

Masada is a play written by Caribbean writer Edgar White, and presented by the Keskidee theatre workshop. Despite the fact that White has two successful productions at the Keskidee to his credit, *Masada* seems to be the kind of play that attracts the attention and funds of cultural bodies such as the Arts Council, but repels the kind of audiences that Keskidee should be seeking to build.

The central theme of the play — that an oppressed people must fight, even to the death, against their would-be masters, is interesting enough to black audiences. White has taken *Masada,* the fortress in which the Jews made their last stand against the Roman Empire, as a supreme symbol of rebellion and resistance. He transports and transforms Masada into a mythical town located in South Africa.

The play is divided into two parts. In the first act some of the characters travel to Masada, and in the second we witness the conditions of life of the people who live there.

The play opens with two of the characters boarding a Masada bound train. One of them, Bancroft, is blind, light skinned, young and heir to multi-millions. His travelling companion, Lazarus, furnishes him with sex, food, intellectual stimulus, human warmth and companionship. When the train crashes, on its way through Europe, Lazarus attempts to shake off Bancroft and run off with a fellow traveller, a pretty girl from Brixton. He is pressed back into service at gun-point by the train guards. They are acting on instructions from Bancroft's all seeing, all knowing, all powerful father.

On reaching Masada we discover that it consists of a huge rubbish dump, around which are clustered the shacks in which the inhabitants of the town live. The talk of the town is the trial and crucifixion of a Christ figure, a saviour of the people.

The play fails to hold the audience enthralled because White's intellectual and literary competence is not matched by a comparable instinctive theatrical flair. In the first half of the play, the relationship between Bancroft and Lazarus is used to good effect to emphasise the writer's views on the way the developed nations batten upon the Third World, but he is reduced, when inspiration apparently fails him, to falling back on characters relating Anancy stories, with no other function, it seems, than to give the play a Caribbean flavour and to fill in time.

The two major images within the play, the smooth running ordered life in Europe symbolised by the train, and the decay and desolation of life in Masada symbolised by the rubbish tip, are bold and imaginative theatrical devices. White, however, does not seem to be able to extend these theatrical metaphors by dialogue, or by any development of character and plot.

White poses the conflicts in Masada/South Africa in the dramatic form of the social realism school. The characters who live in Masada are easily identifiable – the 'coloured' girl with problems of identity and alienation, the black woman who seeks a way out of her horrendous life through the sexual power she wields over men, and the Asian with his particular role in the South African racial and economic hierarchy. In trying to find a resolution for these conflicts, he stumbles into the realms of mysticism and tumbles dialogue, characters and themes all over the stage, leaving one feeling mystified rather than enlightened, not to mention frustrated and finally bored.

Masada is an important play in that White raises many topics that preoccupy blacks. The play touches on the theme of the international nature of the struggles of blacks from Brixton to Bulawayo. It bears on shifting power relations between people of differing classes, sexes and races. But all these strengths within the play are negated by the playwright's lack of theatrical vibrancy and power.

The play is saved from being a total disaster by its director Rufus Collins. He uses actors and stage effects to their fullest advantage. Indeed the sets which were superbly conceived and executed dominated the production, whilst the actors of the Keskidee workshop have developed into disciplined and competent ensemble players. David Haynes, in the role of the friendly neighbourhood leper, is outstandingly good.

Masada points to the dilemma of black theatre in this country at the present time. We have, at least in Rufus Collins, a director of unquestionably high calibre. There is a reservoir of acting talents proven and unproven to be tapped. But there is a dearth of playwrights to develop the capabilities of our black dramatic artists to the full.

January 1979

Frontline Fighter

A documentary film of Reggae Poet Linton K Johnson,
Directed by Franco Rosso

Dread Beat and Blood is the name of a documentary film,
in colour, about the life and work of young Jamaican poet
and political activist, Linton Kwesi Johnson.

It is an unsentimental, sensitive, exciting and thought
provoking cinematic portrait of an artist who, in addition
to having had his poetry published and recorded, is a front
line fighter against the colonization of blacks in British
society. The strength of the film lies in the fact that, in
society today, artists are usually seen as extraordinary
people above and beyond the understanding of ordinary
folk. *Dread Beat and Blood* shows us how Linton has put
his talents at the service of the black working class from
which he comes, and that this background has been a source
of strength to him.

Because Linton is both poet and politico, the film is
divided into two parts. Firstly, the audience is given an
insight into how Linton actually sets about producing his
work. Then, we see him interacting with the people whose
lives provide him with the subject matter for his poetry.

The film keeps our attention at all times because we can
identify with Linton's triumphs and successes. When, for
instance, he is interviewed by a middle class English woman
from LBC, he runs rings around her with a vibrant and
dazzling reading of one of his poems. We feel that his superiority belongs also to us. We are elated that he has established this superiority, not by playing the literary black
superstar, but simply by demonstrating the sheer power
of his talent. Linton makes no concessions by trying to
explain himself or his work to the interviewer, because
it is not to the section of society that she represents that
he wants to speak.

This sequence is just one of many that shows Linton

49

in his role as professional artist. We get further insights into the way Linton produces his works of art, as the camera tracks him during a poetry reading he gives in a small community centre hall. The multi-racial audience is clearly delighted that here is an artist who is willing to come to them rather than having to seek him out in the prestigious surroundings usually associated with an artistic performance.

Even when we see Linton surrounded by the formidable electronic trappings of his art in a sound recording studio, he doesn't try to blind us with the glamour of his position. He tells us that he never imagined, when he was working as a factory hand, that he would ever have had these kinds of resources at his disposal. He makes us understand that he has not always been in the strong position he now finds himself, but has fought and struggled for it as we perhaps could. More informally, we see Linton working with other black musicians in practice sessions. Again, his art is shown to be a part of the ordinary experience of blacks, who have always made music and revelled in verbal play and story telling, and know how to enjoy themselves even when the are working.

Another part of the film deals with Linton as a social being, as well as the artist concerned strictly with a particular art form. This part of the film is particularly interesting as it shows quite clearly how Linton fuses his art with his life. We see him socialising with friends in a Brixton youth club, playing dominoes with them. In a cultural centre in north London, where he worked as a librarian, he discusses, with unemployed black youth, police harassment which he, a rebel youth himself, experienced. When Linton revisits his former school, he coaxes them into questioning the ideas they are being taught at school.

All these people clearly have to respect Linton as much for his integrity and lack of pretension as for his talent as an artist.

Last, but not least, the film deals with Linton's role as a political activist who has a particular point of view on how society should work. At the start of the film we see Linton walking through Brixton market, and as he does so he connects the past to the present by pointing out the parallels between the Brixton he now lives in and Jamaica which he left as a boy of 11. He makes it quite clear that the solid position he now finds himself in − being able to work professionally as a poet — is based on his roots in rural Jamaica, not on the education he received from the British educational system, which thwarted rather than developed his talent.

Some of the most powerful scenes of the film show blacks rebelling and resisting attempts by the British state to destroy their cultural traditions brought with them from their homelands. There is a brilliant and exhilarating sequence showing black youths defeating police attempts to 'mash up' the Notting Hill Carnival. Equally powerful, are the shots of the black community in Bradford, marching in protest against the framing and jailing of an innocent black working class family man. These sequences have not been inserted into the film merely to sensationally illustrate the life and times of a revolutionary black poet. They show the conditions of the lives of the people that inspire Linton's work. As Linton states, he saw a lot of things happening on the streets to blacks, both young and old, and wanted to contribute his talents to their struggles.

Dread Beat and Blood shows us precisely what Linton's contribution to our struggles is. He has fulfilled what is surely the task of the artist in society: to remind us where we are coming from, to tell us the truth about where we are at now, and to point directions in which we best might go. Check out Linton's work, you will find all these elements in them.

The making of *Dread Beat and Blood* is an important event for us, if we accept that our culture is a powerful weapon in our struggle against the movement to colonize blacks living in England. The medium of film, which is able to show every side of a subject, as no other form of communication can, reveals certain important aspects of Linton's life and work that some of us might miss when reading or listening to the poems. The release of the film could bring to a large section of the black community a knowledge of the contribution that black artists like Linton make to our social and political struggles. Hopefully, it is the first of many films that add to our knowledge of our culture, past and present and therefore to our power.

February 1979

Not Quite Enough

For Colored Girls Who Have Considered Suicide When
The Rainbow Is Enuf
by Ntozake Shange
Presented at The Royal Theatre

*For Colored Girls Who Have Considered Suicide When The
Rainbow is Enuf* is a theatrical event developed out of a
series of poems written by an Afro-American woman, Ntozake
Shange. The poems become 'scenes' which add up to a play
whose central theme is the particular form of oppression
experienced by Afro American women and their attempts
to liberate themselves from that oppression.

The subjects the poems cover are the preoccupations
of black women as identified by Ms Shange. The form
of the play consists of seven women reciting the poems
and fleshing out the words with movement, mime, song
and dance. The seven characters reminisce about their child-
hoods and adolescence, agonise about finding a sense of
identity as blacks and as women, and complain about how
badly they are treated by men.

Although there is no plot for the audience to concentrate its attention on, Ms Shange manages to convey sit-
uations and personalities by the sheer force of her extraordinary command and manipulation of language. The
most powerful poem/scene of the production tells the tale
of a Vietnam veteran whose pent up frustrations find release in the killing of his own children during the course
of an argument with his woman. Using just the one actress,
and within a very short space of time, Shange conjures up
a full scale drama with elements of comedy, pathos, tragedy, main actors of different sexes, supporting cast and
the various geographical locations in which the action takes
place.

I found the play highly entertaining because of Shange's amazing gift of the gab, and the skill of the actresses, a bevy of goodlooking women dressed in eyecatching costumes who went through their paces with a slick and seductive professionalism. Think of Millie Jackson, add a Phd in literature, multiply by seven and you'd get a fair idea of the tenor of this production.

Despite the technical skills displayed in the production, the whole enterprise seemed to me remarkably and relentlessly frivolous. You can't help thinking that if Shange's characters concerned themselves more about the conditions that create the infuriating characteristics of the men who are targetted as the women's main oppressors, and less about the relatively trivial trials and tribulations of their domestic, social and romantic lives, these characteristics could be eradicated as a first step towards liberating themselves from an oppression of which the particular forms focused on by Shange are only a part.

The play's finale, which had each woman sanctimoniously intoning 'I found god in myself and I loved her fiercely,' had this black girl considering (given the play's obsession with the way men put down women emotionally and physically) a woman would do better to find a black belt karate champion within herself and train her assiduously; which only goes to show how catching frivolity is.

November 1979

Land of Dreams

Throne in an Autumn Room
by Lennox Brown
Presented at the Keskidee Centre

Throne in an Autumn Room is a most fitting production
for staging at the Keskidee – London's leading venue for
black drama. The subject of the play concerns the effect
of migration on the lives of West Indians.

The action of the play is set in an apartment located in
the 'banana belt', the black working class ghetto of a Can-
adian city. The apartment is occupied by the play's three
main protagonists. Tyrell Shabang is an 'unemployed, self-
employed' travel agent. He is also a buffer between his
wife Christine, once a teacher in Trinidad, presently a cook
for rich whites, and Ray a university drop-out and childhood friend of Tyrell's. Ray and Christine are constantly
at war, as Ray's ability to aid and abet Tyrell's grandiose
schemes far outstrips his ability to produce the rent Christine insistently and consistently demands. The relationship
between the three provides Brown with the opportunity
of examining the circumstances of the lives of three blacks,
differentiated by sex and educational qualifications, and
allows him also to deal with the themes of the demoralization experienced by immigrants, their search for identity,
their quest for self respect and need to satisfy basic material needs.

Brown is a distinguished and accomplished dramatist.
Unlike many black playwrights whose work has been shown
at the Keskidee, he is able to express his ideas with a genuine
dramatic flair. Tyrell and Ray's demoralization is conveyed
not merely by dialogue, but by way of the plot Brown has
chosen.

The plot turns on Ray's desperate efforts to keep a roof

over his head. Christine may be Queen in the apartment due to her earning capacity, but whilst she is out at work, Ray plots an apartment revolution. Christine returns home one evening to find her living room transformed into the throne room of the play's title; Tyrell resplendent in a carnival king's costume from happier days, and Ray hovering about nervously in a dashiki. With good reason, for he is responsible for the bizarre spectacle. What Christine witnesses is, in fact, a dress rehearsal for a fantastic fraud Ray hopes to perpetrate. Having discovered from a newspaper photograph that an African king is the spitting image of Tyrell, Ray decides to win respect and gain money by exploiting the likeness.

Brown's theatrical inventiveness never fails him, and this is amply demonstrated in the scene in which Ray's skank is sussed when he and Tyrell 'go public' on a TV programme. All the themes within the play — the duplicity and subversive dominance of whites, the powerlessness of blacks and the idea of Africa as motherland are tied up in an ingenious and hilarious climax.

Tyrell behaves like a giant spanner in the works of the electronic and intellectual precision of the TV programme. Abandoning Ray's carefully researched script, Tyrell draws on his street sense, and ad libs in a most unkingly fashion, thus winning from the supercilious white interviewers an awe he never commanded whilst posing as cousin, several times removed (by time and space over the centuries) of an African king.

Rufus Collins' direction, as usual, matches the play's excellence. His handling of the TV sequence, for example, is imaginative and innovative, developing and enhancing the satirical mood of the scene. Henry Mutto's design and decor, particularly in this scene and of the production in general, must also be highly commended.

The actors, playing parts they can really get their teeth into, give superb, performances. Anton Phillips conveys the disarming charm of the thorough-going scamp that Ray is with utter conviction. Yvonne Giddens, with her mobile and expressive face, combines a talent as a fine comedienne with skill in the straight acting required for in her role as the realist of the trio. Lloyd Anderson as Tyrell achieves the transformation from a '45 year old failure' to the self important 'pretender' to the throne without letting his character degenerate into a caricature.

Throne in an Autumn Room is an impressive play by any standards. Ideas, dialogue and characterisation mesh in a seamless whole. It is a highly entertaining play, that at the same time raises issues that seriously concern blacks. The Keskidee Theatre Company has often seemed in the past to be in search of an author to develop the potential it has shown. In Lennox Brown it appears to have found one.

November 1979

Coon Show

Three Plays: Gloo Joo/Full Frontal/For the West (Uganda)
Written by Michael Hastings
Published by Penguin Plays, £1.50

Michael Hastings is a British writer whose prolific output (short stories, novels and plays) has won him several awards here and in the USA. As one of these awards is television's equivalent of an 'Oscar', Hastings can be identified as an artist whose work is guaranteed maximum exposure and respectful attention.

In Britain, he has carved a niche for himself as a writer on the subject of race. Three plays he has written on this subject, *Gloo Joo*, *Full Frontal* and *For the West (Uganda)*, received rave reviews in the Press. *Gloo Joo,* despite a recession in the theatre, is currently enjoying a revival in the West End. When it first opened, London's most widely circulated evening paper hailed it as the comedy of the year. *Full Frontal* and *For the West (Uganda),* did not have the popular success of their predecessor; they achieved the intellectual and artistic kudos of being staged at The Royal Court, a prestigious venue for radical and revolutionary drama about contemporary issues.

The plays, which have now been published in one volume by Penguin Books, offer the opportunity of studying what a white writer of great renown has to say about blacks at this point in time.

There is a common structure to all the plays. Hastings presents a black protagonist and the forces ranged against him. In *Gloo Joo*, Meadowlark Rachel Warner is an illegal Jamaican immigrant attempting to evade deportation. How he succeeds in this endeavour enables Hastings to express what he thinks of the West Indian way of going about things. Not very much as it turns out.

His description of Warner's personality and behaviour characterises West Indians as the idiots of the global village, relying on low cunning rather than on a developed intelligence to see them through. By the end of the play, because Hastings has attributed not one admirable human characteristic to Warner, he appears not so much a person, more a performing animal, jumping at his white creator's commands. When, in the play a white character asks Warner, 'You didn't mind me calling you a black bastard the odd time', he obligingly replies 'long as a can call you a white one'. Such a black does not exist in reality. Warner is a figment of an essentially racist imagination and an optimistic one at that.

Gabriel Nkoko, the hero of *Full Frontal* is Nigerian. He is also mad. Discovering that a West Indian has run off with his woman, he decides to join the National Front, the most notorious of Britain's fascist organisations. Much of the dialogue of the play, which is in the form of a monologue, consists of Gabriel hurling abuse at West Indians. To gain entrance to the Front's premises, Gabriel pleads 'I ain't West Indian man. Got dignity man. Don't confuse me now. I'm not jah roots Caribbean dreadlocks man.' Hastings while purporting to show the corrosive and corrupting effects of racism on society in general, uses the course of events in the play to belittle West Indians and their culture in particular. His use of a black character to belittle other blacks is a pernicious device he has already used in *Gloo Joo,* implying, as it does, that racism is not a phenomenon peculiar to white society. Hastings' choice of the NF as the organisation Gabriel tries to join makes a mockery of the fact that blacks are presently struggling against racism in this country in a systematic, disciplined and intelligent fashion.

The last play in the collection, *For The West (Uganda),* contains many themes introduced in *Gloo Joo* and developed upon in *Full Frontal.* Hastings choice of the dreaded Idi Amin as the hero of this play allows Hastings to expand to the full his favourite theme of the black man's inhumanity to the black man. What distinguishes this play from its predecessors is that unlike Warner and Gabriel, Idi is shown resisting rather than accommodating attempts by whites to oppress him. Hastings, however, structures the play to show that Idi's power to determine his own destiny and that of his people is based on delusions. Much of the play's action takes place in a dream of Idi's, as if, for Hastings, the very idea of black power is something that is 'out of this world'.

None of the plays by way of plot, or delineation of character show the slightest respect for blacks. On the contrary, they are a contemporary version of the traditional 'coon' shows and serve much the same purpose. In every one of the plays, the mannerisms and conditions of the lives of blacks are held up to ridicule for a white audience's delectation and edification as blacks do not generally, in this country patronise the theatre. The plays reinforce all the banal, racist stereotypes; that blacks are amoral, immoral feckless, stupid, ignorant and unprincipled. Any white attending these plays must come away reassured that blacks do not pose any serious threat to the continuing supremacy of whites.

December 1980/January 1981

Celebrating Black Culture

Celebrate a Multi-Media Youth Art Festival held at The Commonwealth Institute, March 28 – April 2, 1980

'Celebrate – Multi-Media Youth Arts Festival' is the title of a five day, cultural marathon presented by The Drum Arts Centre in conjunction with the Commonwealth Institute. The Institute's headquarters, a vast and magnificently appointed monument to Britain's colonial past, was invaded by 25 groups drawn from Afro Caribbean communities throughout the country.

The festival encompassed many different art forms – drama, dance, music, painting and photography. However, due to press deadlines, we were only able to cover one day's events, when three dance groups, the Arawak Dancers, Mara Ya Pili, and Ekome performed.

The Arawak Dancers are a group of 14 including a drummer and choreographer. They gave two performances. The first, performed in practice clothes, was a dance class, with the choreographer putting the group through the various routines of classical and modern ballet techniques. Members of the audience, black and white, aged from four to 70, enthusiastically responded to an invitation to join the group on stage.

The second section of the group's performance expressed Caribbean and African themes with appropriate costumes and hairstyles. By this time, the audience included many young blacks, and when they were invited to join the group, they thronged the stage, and totally disregarding the concept of workshop, just got on down and did their own thing with the space and music provided by the Institute.

The distinction between trained and untrained dancers blurred in a joyous celebration by performers and their appreciative audience. What distinguished the former from the latter was that the Arawak dancers have developed the everyday, social and cultural activity of their peers through discipline and organisation into an art form.

Organisation, discipline and skill are also the hallmarks of Mara Y Pili, a 20 strong dance group from the Chapeltown area of Leeds, ranging in age from 10 to 20. Their performance was an impressive feat. They presented a series of dances, inspired by sources as diverse as the poems of Linton Johnson, a photographic essay of the lives of the Nuba of Sudan, the Trinidad Carnival and modern ballet.

The group imaginatively recreated the body decoration peculiar to the Nuba, whilst the modern ballets were excellently designed and conceived, combining elegance and grace with witty sophisticated visual jokes.

The evening culminated in a performance by Ekome. This group is semi professional, supplementing its income by educational demonstrations and government grants. Their performance, as befitted a group, some of whom have 'professional' dance training and who had graduated from amateur black dance groups, represented a flowering of the rich cultural activity that has taken root in our communities. The company of nine gave an utterly enthralling and enchanting performance. The five dancers executed traditional West African dances to the accompaniment of the musicians using African instruments. Apart from the ravishing dancing, we were treated to jokes and thrills. One dance was performed on broken glass.

'Celebrate', from the few events I saw, provided an eye-opening, educative and stimulating view of the life enhancing, cultural activity burgeoning in black communities. It informed us of the existence of blacks in Britain, sure of, and taking an intelligent interest in their African heritage and Caribbean cultural traditions. It showed a community with the strengths to meet new challenges and the willingness and ability to explore and master new techniques. It demonstrated, above all, a black community confident and stable enough to take time out of their working lives to organise, build and develop their own independent institutions geared to serving their particular needs and interests.

May 1980

Hairy

The Disappearance
by Rosa Guy
published by Victor Gollancz, £4.50

Novelist Rosa Guy is Trinidadian born but Harlem raised. This duality of background is reflected in her latest novel: *The Disappearance.* Guy uses the contrasting vernacular speech and life styles of Afro Americans and West Indians like warp and weft to weave incident, dialogue and character into a dense, vivid tapestry depicting the lives of blacks in contemporary, urban America.

In this, her third novel to be published in Britain, Guy continues a theme present in the previous books: the attempts of adolescents to come to terms with a bewildering and menacing adult world. Writer that she is, Guy, in this novel, substantially varies this theme. She shifts in emphasis from a girl's eye view of the world to a boy's, and the form of the novel is that of the thriller.

The book contains the classic ingredients associated with this genre: suspicion and suspense; the cracking of clues and codes; mounting terror and tension as events jigsaw inexorably into place culminating in a startling and dramatic finale.

The locale of the story is the melting pot of New York, simmering in which, amongst others, are communities of Afro Americans and immigrants from the Caribbean. Things boil over when 15 year old Imamu, born John Jones, leaves his apartment in a stinking tenement block in Harlem and goes to live with a West Indian family – the Aimsleys – who own a house in the 'green smelling heaven' of Brooklyn.

'We must act right away,' her mother said or else that poor boy will be taken away from the detention centre after the trial and be sent to one of those places' It hadn't been until after her mother had made all the arrangements for the Aimsleys to be a foster family that Gail – and probably her father – had paused to wonder what was wrong with the boy going to 'one of those places.' However, for Imamu, the transition from Harlem to Brooklyn proves to be not so much a safe deliverance as a leap from the frying pan into the fire.

Fingered in Harlem for murder, he is blamed in Brooklyn when a member of his foster family disappears. The 'street dude' discovers that the attitudes to be found amongst blacks living in a suburb, one rung up from the ghetto, are no less dreadful in consequence for him, than the attitudes to be found in a downtown police station: 'where a young black or Puerto Rican cat could be suffering from diarrhoea of the mouth, or dead, in half an hour.'

With this book Guy's achievement is not merely to have devised an exciting mystery story, but to have raised, within the scope of a highly entertaining work of fiction, issues that are of interest to blacks concerned with struggle against oppression. The theme that blacks cannot 'buy' the power to determine their own destiny, but must fight for it, runs like a vein through the story. Imamu is hero of the book, not just because he solves the riddle of the disappearance of the book's title; he is also the only character in the book, seasoned by a life of deprivation and disadvantage, capable of questioning, analysing and resisting to any great effect, the oppression that shadows the lives of all the characters.

From beginning to end the book compels attention. Apart from arousing in the reader a desire to discover who 'dun' it, the author has created an irresistible and fascinating bunch of characters. These range from a precocious, toothless eight year old to a real West Indian 'tanty' who, with luscious looks, a sharp tongue and meddlesome ways, keeps her wide circle of acquaintance in a constant dizzying spin. Focused though the story is through the experience of blacks, it nevertheless has universal appeal, touching, as it does, on aspects of common human experience – the passions generated by differences between people of age, sex, class and culture. The novel is charged with sex. Guy's subtle and witty treatment of this subject is not marred by the least hint of sentimentality or sordidness. She uses humour throughout the book in an unerring, audacious

63

and graceful manner to drive points home without in any way diminishing the seriousness of the issues dealt with.

In the hands of a less talented writer, the subject matter of the book — the conditions of the lives of a specific group of blacks at a particular point in their history — could have been presented in the form of sociological reportage padded out with descriptive passages. Guy avoids this sterile formula by an imaginative and inventive approach to themes within the novel. Her choosing to make the disappearance of a character central to the novel is a master stroke. This circumstance provides more than an intriguing core to the novel. It becomes a metaphor, brilliantly sustained, for the seemingly inexplicable and insoluble problems blacks have to contend with in American society. The cause and effect of the disappearance are plotted in such a way as to pinpoint and illuminate the cultural, social and political strengths and weaknesses of the blacks whose lives are recorded so faithfully and vivaciously in this book.

November 1980

Paper Dragon

Mama Dragon
A play by Farrukh Dhondy
Presented at The Factory

Mama Dragon is the first play by Farrukh Dhondy, well
known as a political journalist here and in his native India.
He is also a teacher, political activist, author of short stories
and a novel. Infuriatingly and disappointingly, the play in
no way fulfills the promise of its author's background.
Artistically and politically, it is as much a paper dragon
as the 'Mama Dragon' of the play's title – a military machine
which proves to be a potential danger to its would be users
and, in the event, totally useless.

The setting of the play is a government funded project
meant to serve the needs of blacks in the ghetto. As the
play progresses, the project becomes a microcosm of the
political activity of blacks in Britain. Three distinct ten-
dencies are revealed by the behaviour of the characters
who people the project.

The black youth, who frequent the project, are shown
in a state of rebellion against their parents and teachers
and subjected to police surveillance and harassment. In
control of the project is a meddling, mediating black 'miss'
trying to contain the rebelliousness of the youth by diverting their frustration into harmless, cultural activities.
Her leadership qualities are expressed in her organisation
of the bureaucracy necessary for begging handouts from
the state. The unexpected appearance at the project of
Frankie, a black renegade from the British army of occupation in Ireland, bearing weaponry he has liberated, indicates
the possibility of a black insurrection.

The play purports to deal with matters of great moment
and makes reference to stirring events. Posters decorating

the set describe the radical and revolutionary activities of blacks here and in the States. The names of Mao Tse Tung, CLR James et al are invoked to set the political tempo. Yet the play, in terms of structure of plot, dialogue and characterisation, displays inertia of imagination and ideas, an ignorance of what makes a play vibrant and interesting and an ineptitude of theatrical techniques. The plot is pedestrian, the dialogue arch and pedantic rather than witty or profound; the characters, mere caricatures.

The play as a whole lacks dramatic tension, which only appears, after a sort, when it is learned that the National Front propose to march through the environs of the project. There is nothing in the development of characters before this event to persuade the audience to suspend the disbelief that the people passing through the space and time of the play would be galvanised by the appearance at their window of the unacceptable face of the racist body politic. The youth, we only see organising socially and culturally around their daily experience of racist oppression. The project leader merely talks about organising against this oppression, (there is talk about a legal defence committe for one of the youths) when she's not swanning off to restaurants with her white lover and complaining of black men's inhumanity to black women. Frankie, the fighting man, despite his tough talking image, does not inspire confidence, checking out, as he does, the local talent rather than the security of his arsenal.

The flurry of activity around the NF march is derisory. The youth pathetically collect bottles as missiles for all the world like kids amassing milk bottle tops for some charitable purpose.

The project leaders turn from writing applications for Arts Council grants to drafting mobilising leaflets against the fascists. Frankie, up to now built up as a man seasoned and tempered by the discipline of a modern technological army, turns into a parody of a Kamikazi pilot with his schemes to take on the military might of the state armed with mama dragon − an antiquated hand held flame thrower (the manual for which has gone missing), the A-Z and his cousin, an arty farty intellectual. The undeniable impression given by this turn of events is that political organisation of blacks at this moment in time is a joke and a bad one at that.

66

None of the characters command our sympathy let alone respect. They are shown sinking into and floundering about in a slough of incoherent ideologies and muddled methods of organisation and procedure. Farrukh puts his foot in it and wallows. Throughout the play, dialogue squelches as facetious jibes trying to pass for humour are directed indiscriminately at all shades of race and political persuasion. Cynicism and supercilliousness inform delineation of character rather than sensitivity or acute observation of human nature and motivation. Black women are presented either as sentimentally romantic or as sleazy, shrill, scheming smart assed scrubbers, who when not actively subverting radical activity apply a brake on it. West Indian youth are shown as having rhythm and rhetoric and precious little else, whilst the Asian and white males seem effete in comparison to them. Such characters, coming from the pen of a writer with Farrukh's experiences, are a disgrace.

In political struggle, art and culture exist as fronts. An author who writes a play with the poltical content of *Mama Dragon* situates himself at that front. If, as one of the characters in the play mentions, mama dragon, the flame thrower, represents a recruiting agent to a particular kind of struggle, whom is the play recruiting and for what?

If the play is intended as instruction for the uninitiated, then these will receive a relentlessly frivolous and distorted view of the intervention and contribution of blacks to to British politics. Only our weaknesses appear in this production. Our strengths — the establishment and consolidation of independent, radical and revolutionary institutions — are conspicuous by their absence from this work of Farrukh's. As a black politico and writer, if *Mama Dragon* represents an artistic distillation of Farrukh's experiences then, he has chosen, with a lack of good faith, honesty, authenticity and generosity the worst and not the best of what he knows to be the activities pursued by Asians, their comrades from the West Indian community and their allies from amongst whites.

November 1980

Four Films with Blacks as Subjects

Grove Music and Grove Carnival: films by Henry Martin and Steve Shaw. An Arts Council Film.
Riots and Rumours of Riots: by Imruh Bakari Caeser. A National Film School Film.
Burning An Illusion: by Menelik Shabazz. A National Film School Film.

Films about blacks have tended to fall into two categories: worthless but amusing, high-minded and a bit boring. Now, however, there exists a group of young black directors making films that are as entertaining as they are instructive.

Four of these films, *Burning an Illusion, Grove Music, Grove Carnival* and *Riots and Rumours of Riots,* recently had premieres at the annual London Film Festival.

BURNING AN ILLUSION

Burning an Illusion is a full length feature film, in colour, directed by young Barbadian born, Menelik Shabazz. He has concocted a molotov cocktail of a movie, using the most common-place of plots — boy meets girl — to explode a number of ideas on race, sex and class struggle. The film demonstrates the director's powerful grasp of the art of film making. It is glamorous to look at and stimulates the imagination by its inventive development of the banal plot. His choice of a young black woman as principal character is highly original. She embarks on an odyssey, physically and mentally, which allows the director to describe the manners, customs and preoccupations of young working class blacks.

The meticulous attention paid to details of dialogue, dress and decor, the exquisite matching of actor to character so that not only the 'stars', but the entire superb supporting cast turn in faultless performances, lends the film an authenticity that makes it riveting to watch. Underneath the lush, surface bloom of the film, imparted to it by excellent photography, is a revealing account of the refusal of young blacks to be treated as victims in this society.

REGGAE AND CARNIVAL

Grove Music is a documentary film, in colour, by Trinidadian, Henry Martin. It takes a look at musicians living in 'The Grove', an area in London's Notting Hill where, during the race riots of the 50s, blacks had to fight for their very lives. Various musicians are shown in performance: Black Harmony, Inity Rhythm, Aswad, Sons of Jah, Brimstone and Junior Brown. Also included are interviews with musicians. The musicians state their philosophy — that of Rastafarianism — with its rejection of the mores of European civilisation. The film is a cogent and coherent statement in favour of this section of the black community. Martin makes intelligent and imaginative use of archive material — mostly newsreels — to show what the Rastas are for, and what they have broken from. In one instance, we see a black serviceman from the 40s flanked by white colleagues pledging 'social integration' and 'cooperation' on the part of West Indian immigrants.

We then see members of the following generation — in this case youths from the group Aswad — describing the music they play as music for rebels. Visually, the film is excellent, image is matched to idea vividly and precisely. In a telling sequence he expresses the Rastas belief that they are a nation within a nation. A group of young blacks appear on screen engaged in the typically English occupation of playing football, dressed in kit which flaunts the red, green and gold colours of the sect.

Grove Music demonstrates the power of film to distort as well as record reality. Martin films the Grove musicians so that they appear to be a force for the political and cultural liberation of blacks. This is achieved by the juxtaposition in the film of the musicians to soldiers fighting in Africa and also leaders of revolutionary movements in the Third World like Castro, Nyerere and Grenada's Maurice Bishop.

The film *Grove Carnival* resembles nothing so much as a giant moving picture postcard in glorious colour. Like most postcards, it says little about one of the most attended cultural events of the country's cultural calendar. An event, moreover, which is the major focus for blacks in this country, struggling to establish and develop their unique cultural and social formations against great odds. The film contains spectacular views of the marvellous costumes of the bands and revelry, and makes you wish you were there all over again.

RIOTS AND RUMOURS OF RIOTS

Riots and Rumours of Riots is a colour documentary by Imruh Caesar. In it he alternates lengthy interviews with middle-aged blacks, talking about their experiences in the 40s and 50s, with sequences describing the lives of young blacks in contemporary Britain. The film is remarkable for the prodigious amount of information it disseminates. Caesar brings to light a wealth of material – still photographs, posters, handbills, newspaper clippings and newsreel footage.

These are used to enhance the observations made by the pioneers of West Indian immigration to Britain, and are fascinating in their variety and scope. A recruiting poster shows the patriotic fervour of a previous generation of West Indians for the mother country during the World War II. An advertisement shows how the same people were denied the basics of life – a place to live – by the host community. The film is more than an academic exercise in black history. This year when 13 West Indian children were massacred in a racist arson attack, newsreel footage of the funeral of Kelso Cochran, murdered in the Notting Hill race riots of 1959, transmits shock waves of recognition. The film chronicles the systematic oppression of blacks in this country over the years.

The flames of rebellion and resistance, raging through Britain earlier this year, were ignited and fanned from city to city across the nation by the country's young blacks. This recent crop of films shows they had been a long time smouldering. The films capture and reflect the spirit of insurrection abroad in the black community, and show that despite their settlement in Britain for three decades, and more, blacks cannot be regarded as mere coloured versions of the whites they live alongside. Absent from

70

these films are themes which divert from rather than focus on the issues at stake in the black community. Gone too are protagonists who are a-credit-to-the-race because they display a passive stoicism in the face of adversity rather than a menacing militancy.

December 1981/January 1982

Plays & Playwrights in Black Theatre

A forum on black theatre was held during the First International Book Fair of Radical Black and Third World Books. Two generations of black writers, producers, directors and actors contributed to the debate. Norman Beaton and Pearl Connor described their struggles from the late 40s to establish black theatre in Britain. Farrukh Dhondy, an Asian writer, dispelled the myth that black theatre is still being suppressed. On the contrary, he informed us, the theatrical establishment is falling over itself to commission works by black writers; and indeed, over the last couple of months, plays by Farrukh, Cas Phillips, Mustapha Matura, Alton Kumalo and Edgar White have been staged.

WHERE THERE IS DARKNESS
Where There is Darkness, a play by Cas Phillips, a young writer born in St Kitts, has recently played to critical acclaim at the Lyric Theatre in Hammersmith. The play is based on a maxim from the heyday of West Indian migration to Britain that, 'the quickest way from the gutter to the hills is through London'.

The structure of the play is strictly traditional. Lights go up on the sort of set, (the back patio of a select, suburban villa) onto which one expects, at any moment, a character will bound enquiring 'who's for tennis?' No such polite activity takes place, for this highly desirable residence is the property of Albert Williams, a West Indian immigrant, who has clawed his way to the top. Recriminations, accusations and curses are exchanged in a particularly vicious version of the truth-game played during a party thrown to celebrate Albert's realisation of the Great West Indian Dream. He is retiring to the Caribbean.

Phillips has crafted this play solidly, with its well conceived plot and imaginative theatrical devices. The retirement party brings together various members of contemporary society. Hostess to the party is Albert's second wife, she is young, middle class and white. His undergraduate son, from an earlier marriage to an island girl, arrives late at the party. He has a girlfriend from the beads and braids brigade in tow. Appearing in vignettes that conjure up his past life in the Caribbean and early days in London, are Albert's first wife, the white woman he 'graduates' to on his crash course to the top and a fellow immigrant, formerly his mentor. All of these Albert has used, abused and discarded. Phillips shows Albert's victory over his humble, immigrant beginnings to be a hollow one. Characters from his past and present emerge like so many grubs eating through the facade of his life, seemingly as polished as the surfaces of his home.

The play works well on several levels. It raises issues that are crucial and relevant to the black community: the pains of exile and dreams of exodus, the struggle on the part of black men for manhood, and on the part of black women for liberation from the double oppression of being black and female.

Albert is cast as a leading race relations industrialist which throws the audience into the debate of how the growth of that industry has dissipated and corrupted the initiatives and energies of blacks.

The pitting of one generation against the next, men against women, black against white, working class values against those of the middle class provide for lively entertainment as the players exchange rallies of observant and often sharp repartee. The use of 'flash back' scenes place contemporary issues in their proper historical context.

The strengths within the play are seriously undermined by Phillips' weak development of his characters. They are not much more than well researched stereotypes and seem somehow too lightweight to bear the burden of the themes within the play. Their reactions to any development to the plot were so predictable that there was little dramatic tension during the course of the evening. Ultimately, one felt that the characters spring not from Phillips' intimate grasp of the predicament he places them in, but from the tip of his pen.

TRINITY

Edgar White's play *Trinity* is stimulating and intelligent. It is made up of three one act plays, perfectly cast and finely acted.

In *Man and Soul,* the first playlet, White tackles the theme of Carnival. He avoids treating the subject in a trite manner by focusing the event not through the relationship of police/black youth, but through the relationship of two youths, an African and a West Indian who have been raked off the streets and into a detention cell in Notting Hill Police Station.

Both have been divided culturally, socially and educationally over the centuries. This division is sharply illustrated by their different reactions while in detention. The African rolls out his prayer mat while the young West Indian busies himself with constructing a marijuana joint. They, nevertheless, establish a unity forged in the heat of the politics of Carnival.

The second playlet, *The Case of Dr Kola,* concerns the corrupt practices of the ruling elites in Africa. Here, again, White avoids a banal treatment of this subject, using a dry wit and humour to drive home some serious political lessons. The humour of the piece depends, not on the fact that a West Indian actor is 'taking off' an African accent, but from White's keen powers of observation and ability to create an authentic, African type rather than a clumsy caricature. Kola, a deposed government minister, has death, in the shape of a young army officer, staring him in the face. Still, he finds time to pompously and arrogantly muse on the fact that he, a professional man, should have been brought so low by a mere illiterate, his wife. Her only words of English are 'Harrods' and 'credit card'.

That Generation is a beautiful piece of theatre. With just three players and one simple set, White captures, in spirit as well as in words, the world of an immigrant travelling from Trinidad to London in the 50s. Once again, White approaches this well worn theme from a different angle to the norm. Wallace, the chief character of this piece, leaves Trinidad not out of any material necessity, but out of the necessity to escape the stultifying social and cultural environment of colonial, island society.

The relationship between Wallace and his wife, Phyllis, is also very different from the usual portrayal of black

74

male/female relationships. It admits of affection, companionship and common interests. I shall remember, for a long time to come and with pleasure, Beverley Martin as Carol, Phyllis' friend, delicately indicating 'when' as Phyllis laces her tea with rum, on what is obviously a typically depressing English winter afternoon.

MEETINGS

Meetings, by Mustapha Matura, is set in Trinidad and shows the two worlds that exist uneasily side by side on the island Hugh, a wealthy contractor lives with his wife Jean, a succesful advertising executive. They inhabit a luxury house complete with swimming pool and space-age kitchen. As Jean is far too busy to lift more than a finger to dial the local take-away for fried chicken, Hugh decides to hire Elsa, a country girl, to cook 'real, old Trinidad food'. Jean, with her straightened hair and fur coat, symbolises the Trinidad that is urban, Americanised and obscenely wealthy. Elsa, with her head tied and faded, cotton frock, personifies a Trinidad that is rural, African and poverty stricken. Hugh finds himself pushed to make a choice as to which of the two worlds he will live in.

Matura seems to be in as great a dilemma as his hero with this play. He can't seem to make up his mind whether it should be a light satiric piece or a tragic work to be taken seriously. The jokes about the merits and demerits of junk food sort very ill with the development of the plot in which an advertising campaign Jean is spearheading has tragic consequences not only for her life but for the lives of the entire population of the island. Although the play makes valid points about the decadence and degeneracy of the ruling class in the Caribbean, they are submerged in all the Trinidadian in-jokes about food which for non-Trinidadians soon becomes tedious and boring. It was an inventive and original idea to focus this tale of low living in high places through the eating habits of the protagonists. However, it is an idea more suited to a sketch than to a full-length play.

Black theatre seems, at present, to consist of black writers producing plays dealing with subjects that preoccupy blacks for black theatre companies to perform before mainly white and middle class audiences at established theatrical venues. It seems an inescapable conclusion that blacks working in theatre are unconcerned that a black audience does not exist for their work. This leads them to equate, with progress, gaining a toe-hold with a play here and there in the established theatre of the country. Progress it is not. A vibrant and alert audience awaits them in the black community. It is for these writers to activate and inspire this tremendous potential. After all Ngugi Wa Thiongo did it in Kenya.

May/June 1982

Dreadful

Countryman
Produced by Island Films

'Jah would never give a power to a baldhead
run come crucify the dread......',
wrote the late, great Bob Marley. How ironic that Island Records, who promoted his work, should have produced the film *Countryman,* which exploits the image of Rasta, to the sect's detriment and their own commercial advantage. For apart from the soundtrack, contributed by artists from the Island stable, the film has very little merit.

Because of the political nature of much of reggae music, the film has been cast in the mould of a musical political thriller. When, for example, Countryman, the hero of the film rescues two witless white American hippies who tumble and stumble into the geographic and political jungles of Jamaica, the trio gorge themselves on the fruits of the island to the strains of *Pass It On.* Throughout the film other such golden oldies set the mood for the scenes.

In recognition that not all who groove to the rhythm of the music will necessarily dig its blues, the dynamic elements of the plot, which concern the violent struggle for power between government and opposition during the last elections held in Jamaica, are diluted with a syrupy sub-plot romanticising the lives of the island's Rastas. Lured by the prospect of hard music, the captive audience has to endure a soft scenario.

The producers of the film make the great claim for it that it was inspired by the words and music of Bob Marley. Strange then that it should be derivative, sentimental, shallow and tedious. Script, direction and acting are distinctly lacking

77

in lustre. *Countryman* is a highly conservative film. It comes from a long line of films depicting blacks as superstitious savages. Countryman, with clouds of ganga trailing about his glamorous locks, not to mention his tendency of being of service to whites in distress, is merely the noble savage updated to the 1980s.

If my review does not reveal a coherent plot for the film, it is because there is none. Alas! Poor Marley, he deserved a better epitaph than this.

August/September 1983

Apartheid Without Tears

Woza Albert!
Presented by The Market Theatre Company, Johannesburg
Performed At The Riverside Studios

Watching a performance of *Woza Albert!* is like taking a crash course in apartheid.

The play is short and deals with the basic economic, and political structures of the system. There is much repetition of material, with characters and events rehearsing twin themes of repression and resistance. It is comprehensive in scope; pass laws, the so-called black homelands, persecution of political dissidents and the continuous history of black rebellion from the days of the Zulu warrior kingdoms to the present are described in detail.

Given the level of repression in South Africa, it is no wonder that Percy Mtwa and Mbongeni Ngema co-authors and performers of the play should have conceived it as an allegory – one based on the events occurring when Morena, a Christ figure, chooses South Africa as the venue for his return gig. The plot allows for satiric comment on the ruling regime's tactic of recruiting international superstars as apologists for apartheid and the country's image of herself as a last bastion of Christianity. The familiarity of the theme ensures the play's appeal to a mass audience.

The simplicity of the play's concept is carried through to its staging. Two actors using the minimum of props – a couple of tea chests and a rack of clothes for lightning changes of character – conjure up South African society in its entirety.

Mtwa and Ngema impersonate a cross-section of the population – the women, men and children, black as well as white – Morena encounters on his progress around the country. The sounds and sights of the environment are also recreated to good effect. In a notable sequence about

Albert Street, where work passes are issued, the stage seethes — black men run alongside speeding cars, scrapping like dogs over jobs casually offered them through car windows by white men. The havoc wreaked by the pass laws, the arbitrary nature of the power wielded by whites and the degredation of the work on offer are powerfully conveyed. This scene, however, is exceptional, most of the others work against the play fulfilling its potential as a swingeing attack on apartheid.

A programme note acknowledges support for the play (in South Africa) 'from all economic levels of the public at large', including, presumably redneck Afrikaners. As if wary of exposing the iniquities of the system, Mtwa and Ngema pander to the audience with the nervous assiduousness of teachers faced with the bottom stream in the local neighbourhood Comprehensive. Song and dance routines, hugely diverting mime sequences and knockabout comedy are used to cheer up the tedious facts of life under apartheid.

The finale consists of Morena resurrecting the fallen heroines and heroes of resistance to the regime (amongst them Luthuli — the 'Albert' of the play's title — 'Woza' means arise). But this note of militant triumph comes at the end of a long haul, during which blacks are portrayed, in the main, as mere victims of the system, to be patronised and pitied; rather than as protagonists to be feared and reckoned with.

Black schoolchildren, in 1976, forced the government to accede to their demands. Yet the character chosen to represent them, as played by Mtwa, comes over not so much touchingly naive as touched in the head — a vindication one would have thought of the government's reluctance to fund education for blacks. A scene in which a pathetic 'old girl' rummages through the dustbins of whites focuses attention on the unequal distribution of the country's wealth. The spectre of a violent seizure of power by blacks is raised in a scene in which Ngema, playing a befuddled tramp reminisces about the days when Dingane, son of Shaka, carried out a highly organised massacre of whites. It is a virtuoso performance. The young actor, all quavering voice and trembling limbs struggles throughout this monologue to thread a needle to patch a threadbare coat. His eventual success stops the show. The applause was not so much for the sentiments expressed in the scene as for the actors poignant representation of an artful old codger. Ngema produces no theatrical fireworks in his portryal of Zulu Boy, a modern militant. When this character jettisons his pass book, the audience never even noticed, or, if they did, chose not to applaud. There's not a bad nigger in the entire cast to darken the atmosphere of sweetness and light generated by the play.

This eagerness to sweeten the bitter facts of life lived at the tip of the boot of apartheid is shown in the use of ping pong balls as false noses to denote white characters. It is an ingenious theatrical device, but also has the effect of transforming such characters, as in the case of the prison guards, into harmless and endearing clowns. It is as if Mtwa and Ngema believe, that, as black artists aspiring to criticise whites, they have to be kind to be cruel.

The theme begs for satire at its most corrosive and wicked parodies of selected targets. Instead, Mtwa and Ngema, with the assistance of Barney Simon, a white member of the company, provide a series of groan-inducing jokes. A jail in which Morena is detained, and from whose upper storeys (in the great South African tradition) he is hurled, but borne aloft by angels, is described as lacking an A.A. device. Geddit? If so, you deserve a free ticket to the show. The lameness and tameness of the dialogue, in striking contrast to the physical skills displayed by the actors, reinforce the stereotype of blacks being all brawn and no brain.

Woza Albert! is not an example of creation for liberation, but rather an act of collaboration with the South African authorities. It is a cultural artifact built to government specifications and suitable for export to promote an acceptable face of apartheid. Like the busy, laughing, dancing niggers on the plantations of old, the play serves to reassure the masters of South Africa that they face no immediate threat from their blacks and convince the visitor/audience that the situation in that country isn't as dread as her de-detractors claim.

January 1983

Over the Top

Beyond the 'A' Penny Steps
A play by Tony Dennis
Presented at The Trycycle Theatre, Kilburn

Plays written by black authors are now staples of the diet offered by fringe theatres of the more established sort. An example of this trend is the production *Beyond the 'A' Penny Steps*, which opened in June at the Trycycle Theatre in Kilburn.

The play is also part of another cultural phenomenon. It matches almost character for character a number of other plays recently performed on the London stage written by West Indian authors. The theme of these plays concerns the different ways generations within a single black family cope with surviving in a society with the odds stacked against them. It is no coincidence that these plays have emerged at this point in time, in a decade whose opening years have been marked by blacks taking to the streets to protest and engage in open warfare on a massive scale. Some twenty years ago in America, during the period of the black power movement, Lorraine Hansbury wrote a play which is a classic study of blacks caught in transition between old and new values and a shift in the political climate. The play took its title, *A Raisin in the Sun*, from a Langston Hughes poem and is a response, as is *Beyond the 'A' Penny Steps*, to a number of questions asked by it.

One would have thought, given Tony Dennis' background (he was born in Jamaica and raised in Britain) that he would have displayed some authority, sensitivity and authenticity in his treatment of the theme. Not a bit of it. The play comes over like a 3D version of a shock horror expose in a cheap tabloid on the burning issues of our times — the youth of today! the new woman! racial prejudice!

Mr Dennis, who wrote for the papers before writing for the stage, presents us with a series of characters and events as eyecatching and mind boggling as a headline. Having thought up the headline, it is as if Dennis has difficulty writing the column. His way round this obstacle is to treat every incident in a sensational manner.

Mark, the son of the house, gets involved in the attempted robbery of an elderly white woman, which results in her death. Not only is she raped, but the lighted bulb of a standard lamp is applied to the soles of her feet. It has been established that Mark is unemployed, a man of leisure who could take time. But are we really to believe that a youth who slurps orangeade from a tin goes in for these sorts of refinements? Dennis indulges his taste for the cheap and nasty throughout the evening. The son is not the only member of the family with a skeleton in the cupboard so to speak. The rest of the family come clattering forth at regular intervals. Mother Carmen, professional nurse and devoted wife and mother, regrets the love of her life, a red-skinned man she abandoned to marry Burt, a black-skinned man who was about to hit the road to Britain and prosperity. Burt, seemingly the stalwart head of the house, scared stiff now the boom-time of the 60s has dissolved into the recession of the 80s, is secretly planning to retreat to the West Indies. Daughter Yvonne fails to introduce her boyfriend to her parents because he is white, not, as they fondly imagine, because she is too busy studying for 'A' levels. One gets the overwhelming impression by the end of the evening that the tragedy that befalls the family stems from each individual's psychological weaknesses.

The play is structured like a soap opera. The many scenes, far more than in a conventional stage play, are like episodes, complete in themselves, of a long running TV series, with the advantage that you wait only a matter of minutes rather than days to learn the outcome of the numerous crises and cliff hangers. Like any writer of soap opera, Dennis can take for granted his audience's familiarity with his theme. They have seen it all before in Cas Phillips' *Where There is Darkness,* Michael Macmillan's *Night Duty,* Edgar White's *Nine Nights.*

The direction of the play is as slack as ome of the events that take place. When the father beats his son, although the latter is shown dramatically arching his back, the belt

83

could quite clearly be seen making contact with the floor. Stephen McFarlane plays son Mark to evil perfection — a little black cuckoo using the family nest as safehouse whilst on the run from the police. Mona Hammond, real professional that she is, with little assistance from the author, carries off her role as mother on automatic pilot. Judith Jacob as the black in blue stockings, with plenty of assistance from the wardrobe department looks her part. Ruddy L. Davis performs the role of violent paterfamilias in suitably musclebound fashion.

Budding black playwrights like Tony Dennis need to apply themselves to perfecting the skills required for their craft. If they do not, the bandwagon they're presently riding could, once the current vogue for black plays ends, turn into a hearse.

August 1983

Jamaican Theatre

Smile Orange
A play by Trevor Rhone
Directed by Rufus Collins
Presented at the Trycycle Theatre

Rhone sets *Smile Orange* in a down-market, cut-price hotel with all systems awry for the start of the tourist season. The hotel stands as a metaphor for Jamaica and her society. The mulatto assistant manager (the manager is white) is attempting to hang onto the wealth generated by the foreign invaders. He manages the hotel with the desperation of a captain of a sinking ship. All around him his staff are abandoning the heavily listing craft like rats. It's everyone for himself, and the devil take the hindmost – in this instance those hapless tourists who don't know the 'runnings'.

Using the genre of farce, Rhone explodes long held myths. The play shows Jamaica to be not so much island in the sun, as island in the shit; not so much paradise isle as hellhole. He paints an unsentimental picture of Jamaicans, regardless of hue or class, fighting against differing levels of exploitation and oppression by any means necessary and surviving if not exactly winning.

The author is not the only professional involved in this production. Rufus Collins, the director, used to be resident director at the Keskidee, for many years London's leading venue for black plays. The actors, Cassie McFarlane, Anton Phillips, T Bone Wilson, Malcolm Fredericks and Sylvester Williams are either graduates from drama school or have worked solidly as professional actors.

As the hotel receptionist, Cassie McFarlane is as good an actress as she is good looking. She sashays around the hotel like an afro on legs in her crotch-skimming miniskirts.

Her 'Mocha Beech 'Ortel Can Hi Help Yeow?' is more a challenge than a request as she consistently sabotages the assistant manager's calls, whilst making the right connections to her friend to plot and scheme her escape to the USA with a rich tourist. Sylvester Williams, as the countryboy waiter, kills one dead with laughter as he spins round on the spot like a demented ostrich, at one and the same time trying to make himself scarce and inform Anton Phillip's assistant manager that a tourist has drowned in the hotel pool. Not surprising since Malcolm Frederick, as the unscrupulous 'Romeo' on the hotel staff has foisted his brothers-in-law – both non-swimmers – onto the unsuspecting management as lifeguards.

Rufus Collins does not allow the frenetic pace of the farce to degenerate into tedious predictability. He subtly and imaginatively alters the pace and mood in a key scene where the staff join together to outwit management. As if to emphasise the seriousness of the moment, Rufus directs the actors to move in slow motion as they set about meticulously preparing a tray with food and flowers to soften up the assistant manager. This instance of solidarity and comradeship among the staff has the quality of a dream, a mirage, in contrast to the nightmare atmosphere of backbiting and competition that prevails in the hotel.

This production shows the high standards of acting and directing achieved by black artists freed from having to struggle against an inadequate script and given the oppotunity of concentrating on the task of practising their craft. It is a step, at least, in the right direction for the development of black theatre in this country. 'Smile Orange?' I laughed 'til I cried.

October 1983

Inferno

QPH
Performed by Sistren Jamaican Women's Theatre Collective at The Drill Hall

QPH are the initials of the names of three elderly Jamaican women, Queenie, Pearlie and Hopie. All three were living in an almshouse in Kingston when it caught fire in May 1980. Hopie died alongside 166 other women. Pearlie was to die a year later, whilst Queenie survives to this day.

A series of flashbacks reveal that the women have always lived with fire at their backs. Pearlie, the light-skinned darling of middle class parents, is cast out when she become pregnant, shattering all hopes of her making a 'good' marriage. She becomes a prostitute, brutalised on the streets and shunned by her fellow inmates. Hopie after a life time's service in the big house of rich relatives continues to be a slave to others' needs as cook for the other inmates, receiving scant appreciation for doing so. Queenie, strong survivor though she is, has suffered the pain and humiliation of being abandoned by the children and man she has devoted her life to. The women, finally victims of the authorities who run the almshouses, have been victims one way or another most of their lives.

Sistren do not develop their plays from a prepared script, but from improvisation exercises during workshops. This does not mean that the end product is ragged, incoherent and an undisciplined mess. The play is highly structured. The flashbacks tracing the women's journey to that fateful night produce vivid and moving vignettes of the lives of poor and uneducated women in urban Jamaica.

There is one scene in which two of the all female cast appear as ghetto youths complete with tams, shades and ghetto blaster to harass the women. The impact of the scene derives not just from the hilarity of seeing the actres-

87

ses providing a sharply observed and wickedly funny parody of the speech and movements of a couple of bad youths. The sequence powerfully conveys the indifference of a society that resigns the powerless — women and the elderly — to the scrapheap.

The scenes that take place in the women's ward again are entertaining because the actresses have meticulously researched and portray the idiosyncracies of a group of cantankerous characters with great skill. The scene emphasises that the women are not just faceless nonentities but human beings to be valued, with needs and aspirations for a better life than the one they are forced to live.

The play provides far more than an evening's entertainment. Though with its songs, dances, ritual and moments of high comedy it is enjoyable to watch. An official inquest absolved the authorities from all blame. QPH lays the blame where it belongs and ensures that although the women died in obscurity and horrific circumstances, they will not be forgotten.

October/November 1983

Sistren are Something Else

Sistren are an all women theatre collective from Jamaica. The founder members of the group are thirteen working class women who approached a drama teacher, also a woman, for assistance in putting on a play in 1977. Five years on, the group is one of Jamaica's leading professional theatre companies whose work has been acclaimed nationally and internationally.

Sistren (a popular Jamaican term for sisters) emerged from a society in which most women are housewives, unemployed or work as unskilled labourers. Not since the 30s, a period of intense political and social unrest in the island's history, have women organised themselves autonomously to better their conditions of life.

Sistren are something else. They have broken the mould which has shaped the lives of women in their society and have created an autonomous organisation around their own needs and demands as women. An organisation, moreover, that not only enables them to improve their material lot in life, but allows them to engage in work that is creative; work that allows for growth and development both of the group and the individuals within it, and is not mere drudgery.

The collective took root in the climate of 'mild socialism' that existed in Jamaica in the 70s. An era, during which, according to Sistren member, Honor Ford Smith, 'one was able to get a sense of a people's culture really moving forward.' This was expressed in the various art forms, particularly drama in Sistren's case.

Sistren existed in embryo by 1977. That year its core members were working as street cleaners for the Special Employment Programme set up by the Manley government This scheme created jobs for approximately 10,000 unemployed women. The group were also among 200 women selected for training in two week seminars which provided instruction in arts and crafts, making them eligible for posts as teachers aides in schools. They were invited to participate in the annual Workers' Week Celebrations and elected to perform a play as their contribution to the event. They asked a senior tutor at the Jamaica School of Drama to assist them with their project. The collaboration resulted in Sistren's first theatrical production *Down Pression Get A Blow,* which was performed in an uptown venue where it was well received.

With their first public performance, Sistren had arrived, but had every intention of going places. The group formulated four main aims. They would introduce drama to working class communities; create plays which described the situation of women; look at how the day to day struggles of women could be advanced; seek to provide the group's members with an income by forming a cooperative and developing organisational skills. There were two ways in which these aims would be achieved. Plays focusing on women's issues would be produced and drama workshops would be held. Through the latter, drama would be used to make women aware 'that the suffering that they experienced as a result of being mothers, or low-status workers or their relations with men is not natural or inevitable.'[1]

Once a year, at a commercial venue in Kingston, Sistren mount a major production. Although the plays are developed from improvisations during workshops, they are honed and polished to satisfy the exacting requirements of an audience drawn from the middle and professional classes. Take the play QPH for example. The chief characters, elderly female paupers who burn to death in a government run almshouse, hardly conform to the glamorous stereotype of womanhood people usually pay to see. Sistren, however, manage to create irresistible and unforgettable characters out of this seemingly unpromising material.

In order to make the audience aware of the enormity of the tragedy, the withered old pods of the women, as they first appear, are also shown in the bud and bloom of their past lives as girls and young women. This involves the audience in a journey with unexpected twists and turns. There are moments of brilliant comedy when, for instance, a character is put down by the congregation at her church who feel that vice (she is the woman of the 'bishop') rather than virtue account for her position of leadership in the church. There are also chilling moments of suspense and

90

tension. In one sequence, a woman who could find no outlet for her youthful beauty and bottle except in prostitution is assaulted and robbed by a sailor. The scene is so well acted that, although the sailor is played by a woman, the actress manages to make the audience suspend disbelief and not feel comfortingly reassured that they are merely watching a parody of male violence against women.

The collective's discipline and skill was demonstrated not only by the fine performances of individual actresses, but also by the group of women who, chanting and dancing in the ritual of Etu, a traditional celebration of the dead, provided a chorus to the main action. Decor, lighting and props enhanced the action precisely and imaginatively. Wooden coffins in turn serve to set the scene of the homes, churches, nightclubs, market places and finally the almshouse the characters inhabit. Flames painted on a backcloth with a single white orb suspended in front of it are brought to life by a subtle play of light creating a fitting atmosphere of impending darkness, doom and death.

The method of producing a play that Sistren have adopted is summed up in the initial exchange between Sistren and the theatre professional they turned to for assistance. She had asked them what they wanted to do a play about. They had insisted the play should be about the way in which women are oppressed and their organisational responses. *Down Pression Get A Blow* concerned a group of women who form a union, organise a strike and achieve their demands. The actresses did not work from a conventional script written in isolation by an individual and then brought back for the group to work on. A Sistren member, who had worked in a garment factory, gave a personal testimony of her experiences there. From these, plot, character and dialogue were developed during improvisations in drama workshops. This method of producing plays revealed a link between personal experience and political analysis. With their first play Sistren did not consciously analyse the issues raised by it. They simply used people's raw experiences as material for a play that had a gutsy immediacy which appealed to the emotions. One of the developments within Sistren was that as their work evolved, personal experience was still used as the basis for plays, but analysis at a more universal level and research at a more objective level emerged and developed as the group itself did.

91

Down Pression Get a Blow was a blue print for all future major productions both in terms of its subject matter and the way in which it was produced. Sistren have since mounted five more major productions. *Bellywoman Bangarang* (1978) which won a Festival Gold Medal deals with teenage pregnancy. *Bandoolu Version* (1979) concerns young girls joining together to survive the banditry in the ghetto. *Nana Yah* (1979) is a historical drama about a female leader and organiser of the Maroons. *QPH* (1981) which won the National Theatre Critics Award for Best Production and Best Jamaican Play for that year, raised the issue of the neglect suffered by poor and elderly women. *Domestick,* Sistren's latest production focuses on women's role in the labour force.

Whilst engaged in research for the first series of workshops from 1980-1982, which dealt with domestic work (paid and unpaid) Sistren discovered that no documentation existed on the subject. Thrown back on their own resources, they created a short skit based on their own experiences about the problems domestic workers face. The skit was presented to domestic workers and women's organisations who were asked to comment on it. From this commentary Sistren unearthed the central role female domestic workers had, for example, played in the passing of the minimum wage law in the 70s — a struggle that could be traced back to the 30s. In organising the workshops, Sistren realised they would have to design a whole new structure of research and information gathering. They discovered that it was only through the testimonies of working class and poor women throughout Jamaica that they had been able to collect information on crucial issues. Issues that had implications, as in the minimum wage struggle, not just for women but for the entire class of low paid workers.

In 1982 Sistren decided to consolidate their workshop activity with targetted groups of women rather than holding scattered one-off workshops with very many different groups. After a period of in-training in political education and workshop organisation, the collective split into two teams to draw together women for a workshop. A rural team contacted and interviewed two groups of rural women: subsistence farmers who sell produce in markets and women living on a housing estate for sugar workers. The urban team mobilised women from Sistren's home communities and middle class women drawn from the audiences of their major productions. The workshops centred around a skit based on the personal testimony of a sugar estate worker. Although she had been appointed a supervisor, she had fallen foul of the equal pay for equal work legislation. Other people from the world of the central character were interviewed — fellow workers, management and union officials. Elements such as the IMF and the conditions it creates, workers' committees and the state were also incorporated into the skit. The four groups of women who saw the skit and discussed the issues raised by it came up with different solutions as to how the worker could have won her case in accordance with their different class backgrounds and levels of education. After this particular series of workshops ended, participants decided to concentrate on further research, followed by action, on such issues as women and health, domestic work, union organisation and the need for women's organisations to take up and deal with these issues.

The women in Sistren could not be further removed from the stereotype of an actress. They are not super-walking talking dolls wound up and set in motion by others — directors and playwrights — ususally men for the entertainment and profit of others — for the most part also male. Sistren take charge of all aspects of their work. Teams have been set up within the collective to handle finance, workshop organisation, publicity and the secretarial services required to keep a complex organisation running smoothly. General meetings are held weekly to which the teams report.

A team has recently been set up to run a silkscreen studio which as well as producing fabric and costumes for productions, makes household goods and fashion items for selling to the general public. Women are generally found backstage only in the wardrobe and makeup departments. Not so with Sistren. Six of its members are currently attending technical classes in stage lighting.

Plans for the future include setting up a children's theatre project; establishing a resource centre to make available research material to assist poor women; publishing and distributing material (using all media) nationally and internationally.

Sistren are not merely successful artists whose work has enhanced and strengthened cultural life in Jamaica. They are also pioneers whose methods of producing theatre are blazing a trail to liberation. In their own words: 'not just from capital, but from sexual oppression, the oppression of old age, the oppression of race.'

January 1984

1. Fighting on Two Fronts: women's struggles and research. Editor Maria Mies

Undefeated

And Night Fell
by Molefe Pheto
Published by Allison & Busby £8.95

South Africa ranks as one of the most industrialised countries of the world. One of its specialised and most highly developed industries is that of terror, designed to process people into model inhabitants of the republic — creatures resigned to apartheid as a way of life. In the book, *And Night Fell,* Molefe Pheto, an African artist, describes how he was put through the mill by the South African Security Forces but emerged 'unrefined'. Throughout his ordeal he retained all his raw hatred of apartheid and constantly defied his interrogators who broke his body but never managed to break his spirit.

In 1976 Pheto lived in Soweto with his wife and four children. He was a founder member of MDALI (Music, Drama, Art and Literature Institute), an organisation formed by artists from Soweto and Alexandra Townships, black ghettos on the outskirts of Johannesburg. The organisation was part of the Black Consciousness movement that sprang up during the the the mid-70s in South Africa. Members of MDALI, realising that the time had come to stop differentiating between art, culture and politics, formed an autonomous organisaion of black artists independent of white patronage. Because of this militant action, they were marked out for detention and interrogation. Pheto was to spend 281 days in a hell on earth, 271 of them in solitary confinement.

Pheto's account of his experiences puts flesh on the bones of the facts of apartheid. Take for example the system of classifying the population in South Africa according to their racial origins. Pheto's description of the personnel involved in a raid on his home, to find incriminating material, makes one realise that there are not four significant categories of people in South Africa — Black, 'Coloured', Asian and European, merely two. The section of the population that is for propping up the crumbling structure of apartheid, and the section which is for bringing it down.

'The Black one Magosha and Night Pot (Asian) suddenly sprang into life and went into action, the guns they were carrying impairing their effectiveness. Magosha had his gun elaborately slung under his right armpit, its thin white canvas strap-laces criss-crossed his narrow back and shoulders. The Black one moved his from the right-hand trouser pocket and shoved it ostentatiously to his back pocket, the one on his right buttock, for easy drawing if it became necessary. Sons ('Coloured') and Night Pot did some shifting of their heavy metal too. I did not see where Purple Suit (European) kept his.'

The book, despite the fact that it details the horrors facing those who oppose the regime, does not make for depressing reading. On the contrary, it indicates the inevitability of the overthrowing of apartheid. One often gets the impression, from press reports, that all opposition to the regime in South Africa has been effectively suppressed with major political activists either dead like Biko or detained as in the case of Mandela. *And Night Fell*, gives a strong impression of ceaseless struggle carried on daily by ordinary people at their places of work and in the communities in which they live. Pheto himself influenced the music students he taught. There were his neighbours in the ghetto who, following the surprise swoop on his home, would have cleansed his house of any compromising material missed in the initial raid.

During his detention Pheto is assisted by black prison guards who tell him.

'My mother's child, don't worry. We'll bring you papers, new ones everyday, as long as we are brought to clean your cell. We'll even take theirs as we start there, and they don't even read the papers, these things', meaning the police. 'We will also tell our blas (brothers and inmates) to look after you.'

And Night Fell is not merely a catalogue of the betrayals and brutality suffered by an individual, written to arouse pity for his sorry plight and admiration for the fortitude he showed in adversity. The specific details of his capture, imprisonment and release are like jigsaw pieces slotted together by Pheto to form a clear and vivid picture of a society forged by the hammer of apartheid.

January 1984